MW00650904

ETHICS IN TECHNOLOGY

DANTES/DSST* Study Guide

© 2019 Breely Crush Publishing, LLC

*DSST is a registered trademark of The Thomson Corporation and its affiliated companies, and does not endorse this book.

971043019143

Published by Breely Crush Publishing, LLC
10808 River Front Parkway
South Jordan, UT 84095
www.breelycrushpublishing.com

ISBN-10: 1-61433-613-X
ISBN-13: 978-1-61433-613-6

Printed and bound in the United States of America.

DSST is a registered trademark of The Thomson Corporation and its affiliated companies, and does not endorse this book.

Table of Contents

Chapter I: Cyberspace and Privacy 1
   Privacy and Security in Cyberspace 1
   Individual Conduct in Cyberspace 4
   Sharing with Online Communities and Social Networking Services 6
   Government Surveillance 10
   Corporate Uses of Personal Data 11
Chapter II: Domestic and International Security 14
   Domestic and International Regulations 14
   Collection and Use of Personal Data: National Security 17
   Hacking and Counter Hacking 19
   Information Warfare 22
   Cyberterrorism 24
Chapter III: Legal Issues in Cyberspace 26
   Free Speech Issues 26
   Privacy Legislation and Industry Self-Regulation 29
   Intellectual Property 32
   Lawful Access and Encryption 36
   Cybercrimes 37
Chapter IV: Technological Innovation and Ethics 39
   Biotechnologies 39
   Internet of Things 42
   Robotics and Artificial Intelligence 43
   Autonomous Vehicles 45
   Social Justice Issues 49
Chapter V: Professional Ethics 50
   Moral Obligations, Legal Liability, and Accountability of Corporations 50
   Moral Responsibilities of IT Professionals 52
   The Role of the Press 55
   Social Media – Positive Reinforcement and
   Dissemination of Unfounded Information 58
   Net Neutrality 60
Sample Test Questions 62
Test-Taking Strategies 98
Test Preparation 98
Legal Note 99

Chapter I: Cyberspace and Privacy

PRIVACY AND SECURITY IN CYBERSPACE

Cyberspace as we know it in 2019 has been around for a little over 20 years, which can be hard to believe given how it has become a cornerstone of the modern experience in most of the world. There are young people now going to college who have never known a world without the Web. With the Internet being such a pervasive part of people's lives, it is hardly surprising to see how susceptible we are to cybercrime including, but not limited to, fraud, theft, surveillance, and hardware sabotage. Even before we stored and transmitted information online, people had to deal with the potential interception and misuse of their information; military establishments funded encryption research to prevent confidential plans from being discovered by enemy forces; banks set up safety deposit boxes so individuals could secure their valuables and important documents; the government created systems like social security numbers to help their citizens maintain their personal identities to make it harder for fraudsters to find victims (among other things, of course).

Despite so many of our crucial systems being dependent on digital security, considerably little has been done to protect them from those who want to take advantage of them. Here are some of the methods which seek to protect data and systems online:

Passwords: Perhaps the simplest form of security is a password, the idea being that only those who know the password are able to access the account or dataspace. Unfortunately, passwords are typically very easy to break, as most people choose passwords that are far too simple.

Captcha codes: With the rise of bots (digital entities programmed for a specific task) in the cybercrime space, we needed a way to distinguish bots from actual humans. These visual puzzles ask users to perform tasks that bots consistently find difficult. There are several kinds of captcha, and they are constantly being updated to keep up with the advances in bot programming.

Encryption: Encryption was around before we went digital, but the process is the same. The original information, called the plaintext, is mixed up using a cipher. This way, only the authorized parties who have the key can unscramble the information. Hackers can still intercept the information, but they will have a hard time figuring out what it is.

Firewalls: A firewall is a system that acts as a checkpoint between trusted and untrusted sources and your device. Think of it like a gatekeeper. When a signal gets to your device, the firewall checks it against your settings and determines whether it is a risk or not. If it is safe, the signal proceeds. If it is determined to pose a threat, you will be asked if you want to proceed with the action. The firewall may also cancel the action outright if it identifies a specific malware (harmful software) like a Trojan virus, which will infect your device with a surveillance bug.

Authentication: Like captcha codes, authentication is a process by which a system asks you to perform certain actions to confirm that you are human, but they go a step further and also help prove that you are who you say you are. Two-factor authentication is an especially helpful redundancy. You may be asked for your password and to answer your security questions, or to input a code the system will send to you via text or email. Having access to that secondary information proves your identity and validates your request.

VPN (Virtual Private Network): VPNs are like firewalls for your network connections. They make your connection secure by hiding data like your IP address and physical location. Many VPN services also prevent your browsing history from being saved and seen and encrypt most other data sent over the network. Not only does this help keep your personal data safe, but it allows you to circumvent censorship and region blocks, for better or worse.

Some methods, like encryption, serve the dual purpose of protecting your privacy as well. For example, banks and credit card companies do not typically have access to your PIN numbers, because they are encrypted. When you enter your PIN into your online bank login, it is encrypted before being sent to the main server for validation. Unfortunately, privacy is a little more complicated. Privacy is a person's right to keep their personal information, affiliations, beliefs, and actions, free from public attention. They have the right to share that information, or not, with whomever they choose. There are certain situations in which a person's actions or agreements will result in them losing their right to privacy, like if they have committed a crime, for example (see Chapter III).

When discussing privacy, it is also important to consider the many nuances surrounding what is private and public and what rights we have to share certain information. There are a number of debates happening surrounding parents sharing information about their young children, for example. On the one hand, people believe it's fine to share things like funny stories or photos of your children on social media so long as you don't post information like your address or the school they attend. Conversely, there are those who argue this is unethical because that child hasn't consented to this information about them being shared in a highly public space, primarily because they are unable to grasp the implications of the Internet and social media yet. This is a topic we may never reach a general consensus on, meaning there may never be legislation dictating the "right" course of action, so it's important that we are informed about privacy and sharing and carefully consider our actions online.

Privacy online is much more complex than privacy in physical space. This is due to a few key factors unique to the Internet and cyberspace; a lot of information can be gathered at once, it can be spread quickly and easily, it can be stored in multiple places almost indefinitely without fear of major degradation, and the digital nature allows for new kinds of information to be collected. Due to the insufficient legislation surrounding online privacy in the U.S., there are a number of professors and researchers who have come up with privacy frameworks to help guide discussion and action in the sector. One of the most comprehensive is by Helen Nissenbaum, who says that privacy decisions should be made based on two factors which she calls "contextual integrity." Contextual integrity asserts that privacy matters are based on "norms of appropriateness" and "norms of distribution." Simply, based on the context of the situation, consider whether the information is appropriate or inappropriate to share within the current context (norms of appropriateness), and then consider whether the information is appropriate or inappropriate to share across contexts (norms of distribution). Let's look at an example scenario:

You run a large theater club and you're trying to plan a closing party for your current cast and crew. You write and distribute a survey asking questions about what people would prefer to do, if they mind alcohol being present, and what kind of allergies or food preferences they have. You collect all of the results and tally them up to help in your planning. At some point, a cast member not involved in the party planning comes to you asking about another person's survey responses because they want to buy them a gift. Should you share the survey results?

If we use Nissenbaum's framework, the context of this situation is the party planning. You distributed the survey and respondents, through their completion of the survey, consented to you having their information for the purposes of party planning. Together, you determined the norms of appropriateness for this context because they shared with you only what was relevant. Now, this cast member is asking you to examine the norms of distribution of the information. This new context is for the purpose of choosing a gift for another group member. This is different from party planning, and this cast member was not involved in the original agreement. Therefore, the contextual integrity demands that you withhold the survey results for the sake of the person's privacy.

When you sign up for any kind of online account, you are asked to agree to a Privacy Policy or EULA (End User Licensing Agreement) which outlines the expectations for the user (you) and the company with regard to the use of any information you put on that account. However, a vast majority of us do not read through the entire document because it is usually long and full of legal jargon we cannot understand anyway. So, using the example from above, if you as club leader put a privacy policy in your survey explaining that by completing the survey, people are consenting to you potentially using the results for purposes apart from party planning, then anyone who completes it could not technically scold you for giving the information to that cast member. However, people tend to agree that this is an unethical practice, and most will likely not complete your survey with that provision in place.

Privacy Policies are typically harmless, outlining what information the company has access to and what it can use for which purposes, and the user's responsibility to only upload information they have the right to share and that they are comfortable sharing. They usually also require that the user waive their rights to sue the company for a variety of situations and relieves them of liability in those situations. This is where Privacy Policies can get tricky, but that will be discussed more in Chapter V.

INDIVIDUAL CONDUCT IN CYBERSPACE

Despite a recent rise in the number of bots (digital programs designed to act as real individuals online) on the Web, the majority of content creators and users are human individuals. Behind every keyboard is a person with their own life, feelings, thoughts, and beliefs. At times, it can be hard to remember this, as the digital space can act as a divide between people, reducing them to text, photos, or a video clip. So, let's look at how people interact with, and behave on, the Internet. To make discussion easier, the portmanteau netiquette is often used when referring to proper online behavior, so we will also be using this term.

Most users are not out to use the Internet for nefarious or harmful purposes. Instead, they use the Internet to do things like advertise and search for businesses and services, network with friends and colleagues, share and do research for personal or academic projects, create and consume content like videos and art, stay up-to-date with the latest news and gossip, and to laugh at adorable pictures of cats, of course. If someone causes harm through their use of the Internet, social media especially, it is usually unintentional.

Since the Internet is embedded so thoroughly in our lives, most employers and entities now have an Online Code of Conduct, outlining the expectations for their staff and students when they are online. A typical Online Code of Conduct will include provisions such as, "Avoid posting photos or text that negatively impact people's perception of you as a professional as this can reflect poorly on the company." Another common provision prohibits cyberbullying and harassment of any kind. This is important because many companies have internal networks and communicate primarily via email, so it is important that employees understand what appropriate online behavior is, and what isn't. This is a particularly interesting area to look at due to the rise of the text message. Texting, from its inception, utilized shorthand and slang much more frequently due to limited file sizes for sending, and the time taken to type on older phone keypads, where multiple key presses were required to get a single letter. Additionally, texting is typically more conversational in tone, allowing for more flexibility in allowed or permitted behavior. However, texting and emailing are two very different methods of communication, but there are a number of people who do not know proper email netiquette. Emails, especially in a workplace setting, are typically more formal affairs, and so more formal language and structure are typically expected.

Cyberspace can give people a sense of invincibility, so they may do or say things they wouldn't otherwise in real life. Most people are rational and law-abiding citizens, but the moment they are denizens of the Internet, they can bend the rules. It would be surprising to find someone over the age of 20 who hasn't pirated a song or TV show or saved and used an image that wasn't copyright free at least once in their life. These people would never steal in real life, but they find reasons to justify it: "I *would* pay for this series, but it's not available here, so I have to pirate it," "It's only one song and if I bought it by itself most of the money wouldn't go to the artist anyway," or "It's just a background image for my community theater performance, no one is going to notice." These ethical dilemmas are unique to cyberspace due to the ease of getting away with the theft. Proxies and VPNs make hiding your digital signature from copyright enforcers simple, and the overwhelming number of people pirating material at any given time means investigators have to focus their efforts on bigger operations that aim to distribute the stolen IP (Intellectual Property [see Chapter III]).

We mentioned VPNs earlier and highlighted how they can allow you to get around digital censorship and region blocks. This means you can watch content on sites like YouTube and Netflix that aren't supposed to be available in your country due to various copyright, or other, laws. This is an interesting discussion because it means that you are skirting copyright regulations which most people understand to be unethical. However, supporters of the tool say that having access to this content is good for the creators and consumers because it helps build a more cohesive fanbase.

A good example would be John Oliver's late show, Last Week Tonight. The entire show is aired on cable on HBO and they post clips to their official YouTube channel, but some of those clips can only be viewed by those with an IP address from the U.S. If you have a cable subscription to HBO in Canada, you can watch the episodes when they air, but if you miss one and want to catch up you will sometimes find that clips from the episode on YouTube are blocked from being watched from a Canadian IP address, despite the episode airing in its entirety on cable. Of course, this can be avoided by subscribing to HBO GO, but again, that only works in the U.S. A VPN and a FlashRouter will allow you to get that HBO GO subscription and watch your shows without being blocked.

The question becomes, is this wrong? You've paid for your subscription to the VPN and the streaming service, and you're trying your best to support the content you enjoy, but the current systems in place have left you unable to access the material in a more direct manner. In the end, the law hasn't quite caught up to VPN technology on this front yet. However, copyright laws have, and even if you can justify it morally, the word of the law considers this a kind of piracy theft. If you feel like you shouldn't be jumping through these hoops to circumvent copyright laws, then don't do it. But if you are of the mind that if a VPN allows you to pay for a service so you can access your favorite content it is better than pirating it, then go for it. The Internet is changing so rapidly, and certain dilemmas are so new that lawmakers and researchers are still grappling with how to regulate it and what the ethical codes should be. We as individual users have to help shape the future by examining our own actions and moral reasoning when we interact with the online world.

While we are on the topic of blocking things online, let's briefly talk about ads and how they play into ethics and individual consumption of content online. Ads are an easy way for creators to earn revenue from their content that doesn't always come at the expense of their fans. However, advertising online is tricky because according to Statista, 27% of users in the U.S. between the ages of 16 and 34 used ad blockers in 2017, and for 2018, 59% of users said they didn't like having ads play on videos. This isn't surprising considering cable TV is less popular in large part due to the number of commercials that play. Blocking ads begs the same questions as pirating and VPNs; what content should you pay for, and what content should you be able to access for free (as in just the price of your Internet hookup)? Again, this is left up to individuals to decide. Many users choose to "whitelist" or allow sites and channels of their choosing to show ads because the money goes to creators they want to support while blocking everything else. Your personal ethical code will determine your relationship with online ads.

SHARING WITH ONLINE COMMUNITIES AND SOCIAL NETWORKING SERVICES

The social media landscape has changed dramatically over the last 10 years. It's grown beyond merely helping friends keep contact outside of school. In an instant, we can connect with a stranger on the other side of the world, wish our favorite celebrity a happy birthday, or thank a business for their products or fantastic service. Social networking platforms allow communities to grow and have provided environments that resulted in the creation of entire subcultures and new kinds of jobs.

Consider memes, for example. By their very nature, memes are only able to exist because social networking platforms provide a space where they can be created, shared, and shared again. Memes depend on a group of people engaging with the content and perpetuating their relevance. Given the impossible number of memes generated each day, they would all quickly disappear into obscurity if not for the incredible reach and influence social media platforms have. Similarly, a person could not become an *influ-*

encer without the existence of social media, and Instagram in particular. An influencer is someone with a large following on one or more social networks who will make deals with sponsors to exchange money for exposure and endorsement in their content. With this recent rise in Internet celebrities and viral marketing, there are a lot of young people looking to make their living on social media by becoming influencers.

There are ethical considerations here as well, as in some countries, including Canada and the United States, sponsored content does not always have to be described as such, meaning that people may be being advertised to without their knowledge. Furthermore, when sponsorships are not publicly discussed, it can lead to worries about bias in the presented media. Say, for example, that a famous technology reviewer is sponsored by a large technology company to discuss the merits of a new product. If the reviewer doesn't make it clear that the review was sponsored, then the potential bias present goes unknown to their viewers. Unlike typical product placement, this form of online sponsorship is referred to as *native advertising*. Native advertising is any instance in which an advertisement takes the form of the typically expected content on an online platform, potentially disguising its true nature as an advertisement.

The quick and accessible nature of social media has allowed for some incredible accomplishments. Thanks to Twitter, companies and services have been able to track disaster response in real time and more effectively triage rescue and relief efforts. Hospitals and emergency shelters can more easily communicate how much space they have available to emergency services and the general public, which helps to alleviate the congestion and chaos at these locations. If an ambulance team sees that a location has posted that it is at max capacity, they can reassess the situation and go straight to an alternative location. Social media has also made it easy to host massive fundraisers because you can reach a global audience with the push of a button. In 2018, popular streamer Ninja raised over $100,000 for the American Foundation for Suicide Prevention during an eight-hour Twitch stream.

Most social media platforms include some sort of audience engagement method such as likes, followers, and reactions. These systems started out as a way to quickly interact with a post that didn't require stopping to comment, thus fostering more scrolling and greater consumption of content. Over time, they evolved into a contentious part of social media, leading platforms like Facebook to do away with their previous "dislike" button. Studies were finding that people were becoming increasingly attached to their online image, and negative reactions to their content were being internalized to such a degree as to cause episodes of anxiety and depression. These effects are still being studied today, and no platform has yet to come up with the perfect solution. Regardless, compulsive use of social media has shown strong correlations with elevated rates of anxiety, depression, self-consciousness, and even narcissism. One interesting study from 2015 suggests that this compulsion could be related to a theory called the psychological ownership theory. This theory claims that humans have a natural urge to collect and accumulate things. The researchers think this applies to analytics in social media because we are led to "collect" things such as likes and followers. When someone sees a small amount of likes on a post, they could start to feel inadequate or worthless and go to extreme lengths to either get a bigger audience and go viral or engage in self-destructive behavior.

Another, more negative, side effect of social media has been the boom in reactionary behavior online. It is well-known that people feel emboldened online and are more apt to engage in aggressive or risky behaviors. The Internet allows people two levels of removal from situations, in that they are not addressing the other person face-to-face and they can do so anonymously. The result is people saying and doing things they would be very unlikely to do in real life. It is easier to be a bully online because they will never be held accountable for their actions. It is also easier to be a "white knight" online because you have access to the alleged offender right at your fingertips. Companies and celebrities are particularly at risk for this kind of social media shaming because everything they say and do is available for public scrutiny.

At the 2019 Grammy Awards, Drake gave a brutally honest acceptance speech and referenced the subjective nature of the awards by saying that musicians are "playing in an opinion-based sport, not a factual-based sport." A few moments later, he paused and turned to those with him on stage after saying, "I promise you, you already won." The broadcast cut to commercial, but it looked like he was turning back to the mic. Almost immediately, Twitter was ablaze with accusations that they intentionally cut him off to try and censor him because they didn't like that he was bringing attention to the flaws in the awards. Representatives had to release a statement clarifying that they genuinely thought Drake had finished and quickly realized the move might be misinterpreted so they asked Drake, following his speech, if he had anything else to say. Drake confirmed that he was indeed finished.

So, why did people get so angry? It's hard to say, but there seems to be a general attitude on social media that having a Twitter or Facebook account gives you the right, and perhaps even the responsibility, to hold others accountable for perceived wrongdoing. This phenomenon is often referred to as outrage culture and "being professionally offended." Humans have a drive to seek justice and punish wrongdoers and social media is a platform through which anyone can drag a company or person to the proverbial gallows to enact digital prosecution-by-mob. This can be a double-edged sword, though. In some cases, social media can bring much-needed attention to a serious issue and help push for change. But in others, like with the Grammys and Drake, this reactionary approach to justice causes people to act without thinking and creates scandal and anger where there is none.

It is important to understand the ramifications of social media so that you can appropriately engage with them. After all, once something is on the Internet, it exists there forever, even if you think you've deleted it. Website caches (storage), the Wayback Machine, and page downloads or screenshots could mean that your words or images will be accessible by anyone at any time. There is a story about a PR rep named Justine Sacco. She had around 170 followers on Twitter—not many by most standards. Right before she got on a plane to Africa, she tweeted about how she hoped she wouldn't contract AIDS. When her flight landed and she turned her phone back on, she was surprised to see that her Tweet had blown up, and people all over the Internet were calling her a despicable bigot and demanding she be fired for her tone-deaf joke. In the end, she was. A single off-colour remark ended an otherwise promising and successful career all because the Internet decided that she deserved to be punished rather than educated. No one bothered to ask her to explain the joke, and those who defended her, believing it was actually a tongue-in-cheek critique of North American privilege, were attacked just as viciously.

Does this mean you should close all of your social media accounts and never use the Internet again? Of course not. But it does mean that you should think about your social media usage and make conscious decisions about what to post, what to share, what to retweet, and what outrage you want to partake in. These are some tips that experts say will help people make better choices around social media use:

- Public or Private: Decide whether you want to curate your friends and followers or if you want everything to be public. Most social networking sites allow you to set it so people have to request to follow you, meaning your posts will only be seen by those you approve.
- Draft It: Before you post anything, especially something that could be considered aggressive or controversial, save it as a draft and walk away and distract yourself for at least 15 minutes. When you go back to that draft, you may find you've changed your mind and either rewrite or scrap it.
- The Employer Test: Ask yourself if what you're about to post would land you in an awkward meeting with your boss (or future boss). If you hesitate even a little bit, then don't post it.
- Research It: It's easy to get caught up in the moment and want to be a part of something. When you come across something like a comment by a politician, quote from a celebrity, or action of a company, you may find yourself reacting strongly (negatively or positively). Always find as much information about the subject as you can before you engage with it on social media. Sometimes things aren't always what they seem.

It all comes down to remembering the human element. On the other end is a person with their own life and things going on. We all say and do things we come to regret and most of the time we learn from those mistakes and make better choices in the future. Unfortunately, the Internet has provided a place for all of those mistakes to be forever stored and used against you when the online mob comes knocking at your Twitter feed.

Just think, if this person was in front of me right now, would I still say what I'm about to say? If this were me, would I want a second chance to explain myself or apologize? Do I mean it when *I* say sorry? While we all work together on figuring out this new digital society, we have to consciously and carefully choose how we present ourselves online.

GOVERNMENT SURVEILLANCE

Data mining is the process by which corporations and entities gather information on consumers and individuals via online means. As mentioned earlier, most, if not all, online entities have a privacy policy of some form or another. Usually, it stipulates that by using the site or service, you are consenting to the company or agency storing your information and tracking any usage statistics they can gather based on your device or browser settings. To some people, this sounds incredibly intrusive and can make them feel more at risk of identity theft or fraud. For others, this is par for the course and they simply take extra precautions when browsing online (e.g. with VPNs, turning off location data, and frequently changing passwords). For this section, we will focus on how the government, specifically in the U.S., collects and uses data in its sometimes controversial *mass surveillance* efforts.

In the United States, the main agencies responsible for daily surveillance are the Information Awareness Office, the National Security Agency (NSA), and the Federal Bureau of Investigation (FBI). They use a method called wiretapping. Before the Internet, this referred only to the monitoring of phone calls, but today it also refers to online surveillance. Every day, these organizations use a combination of humans and computers to analyze a constant stream of data. This begs the question: is this even legal? According to the Communications Assistance for Law Enforcement Act (CALEA) and other legislation, the answer is yes. Laws and regulations specifically involving cyberspace will be covered more in Chapter II, but for now we will look at general surveillance laws.

The first thing to be aware of is the CALEA does not give the government permission to have a tap on every phone and computer in the country on a whim. The point of CALEA, passed in 1994, requires all U.S. telecommunications providers to make their system easy to tap if law enforcement deem it necessary to gather intel on suspected criminals and typically requires that they obtain a warrant to set up the wiretap. Since then, a variety of laws and amendments have been passed to clarify this process and adapt to a changing social digital landscape. The terrorist attacks on September 11, 2001 caused President George W. Bush to pass a controversial amendment to the Foreign Intelligence Surveillance Act (FISA) called the Protect America Act of 2007. This bill, which has been renewed regularly by sitting presidents, most recently in January 2018 under President Donald Trump, removed the warrant requirement for wiretapping surveillance. However, this only applied to cases where the target was in contact with foreign terrorism suspects, U.S. citizen or otherwise. This provision would not apply in cases where the target and suspect were both still in the United States, otherwise known as domestic terrorism. According to Section 702, the agencies in question are legally required to inform citizens if they are currently under surveillance, but several civil rights groups have noted that this notice is often neglected.

Whistleblower Edward Snowden complicated this knowledge in 2013 by leaking classified documents regarding a program codenamed PRISM. PRISM requires U.S. Internet providers to hand over data pertaining to specified searches to the NSA. What this means is if an IP address is recorded making numerous searches for terms like "bomb building," "terrorism," or "government building blueprints," the ISP (Internet Service Provider) has to give that IP address and all related information to the NSA so they can investigate the situation and monitor the individual. This allows security agencies to build comprehensive terror watchlists and hopefully prevent attacks. However, the fact that this information is stored and monitored by ISPs at all is controversial, because it contains the potential for personal information unrelated to national security to be leaked.

One of the biggest groups striving to hold the government accountable and keep their surveillance in check is the American Civil Liberties Union (ACLU). They are a group of staff and associate attorneys who specialize in cases involving the violation of privacy and civil rights. They have filed numerous complaints, Freedom of Information Act (FOIA) requests, and legislative challenges surrounding government surveillance and abuse of power and are instrumental in bringing awareness to these issues. Amnesty International is another group dedicated to human rights and liberties. They conducted a survey in 2015 that showed less than a quarter of the U.S. population is fine with the government spying on them. Amnesty International asserts that the response to government surveillance shouldn't be, "If I'm doing nothing wrong, I've got nothing to hide," but rather, "If I'm doing nothing wrong, why is my privacy being violated?"

In the end, government surveillance is a complex and controversial subject that is constantly evolving. It is important that people educate themselves on current surveillance practices and to be aware of their rights as citizens. While most people will never be wrongfully accused of crimes or inconvenienced (such as being put on the no-fly list) based on mass surveillance, they should still be aware of the issues so they can make informed votes when legislation is proposed and advocate for positive change in the sector, whatever that looks like to their personal beliefs.

CORPORATE USES OF PERSONAL DATA

The landscape of business and marketing has changed drastically since the start of the World Wide Web, and one of those changes is *data-driven marketing*. This refers to the practice of collecting and analyzing consumer data to gather insights to guide marketing and brand decisions. Back in the first section of this chapter, we briefly addressed Privacy Policies and how they can affect your privacy online. They are especially relevant here, as we get into corporations and how they use data collected from users and customers. First, we will look at the kinds of data corporations tend to collect and the methods by which they do so. Then we will discuss what they do with that data and the potential legal or ethical ramifications.

When it comes to data, there are two main categories: *explicit* and *implicit*. Explicit data is information that is clear and stated directly (e.g. your name, your email address), whereas implicit data are conclusions suggested by patterns in the rest of the information. Data mining is controversial because it deals primarily with implicit data. This data is typically assumed to be nonconfidential and therefore public because the conclusions are drawn from accessible information and activities. However, if we consider it from the point of view of Amnesty International then the problem is with the intrusion itself and not the data gathered. We'll come back to this.

The simplest way for corporations to collect data on their customers is to just ask them for their basic information by creating an account. Many corporate websites, in particular those offering goods and services, suggest or require creating an account to use their online portals. You will be asked for your name and email address and sometimes for credit card information and billing/shipping addresses if the site sells products. Often the account will also have optional information for you to fill out such as your gender or marital status. It is usually up to you if you use your real information, or a fake name and spam email account, but for sites that you plan on ordering from, your profile has to match your billing and shipping information. If they don't match, you may experience difficulty in processing transactions or receiving your packages. All of this contributes to their collection of personal data. This is data that is specific to you as an individual customer and can help the company tailor offers to be more relevant to you, as well as send you your orders.

Companies will also make use of surveys. These surveys can be about your satisfaction with a recent experience or purchase with the company, your purchasing habits and preferences, your opinion on new products and marketing campaigns, or anything else the company may want to know. Sometimes, these surveys will come with an offer such as a coupon or chance to win a gift card as incentive to complete the survey. These contribute to a corporation's collection of consumer data. Consumer data helps companies track market trends, buying habits, and guide their advertising, among other things. It also contributes to customer engagement, because the return rate and quality of answers of the surveys tells a company how engaged their customers are with their brand after a purchase.

Sometimes, companies won't even ask you directly for information, but gather it passively from your activity on their site or in stores. This is where careful reading of Privacy Policies is important. When you create an account with a company, you are creating a method by which they can track all of your purchases and interactions with them. Those could be purchases, searches, forum and comment posts, and reviews. All of this information is stored automatically, and many Privacy Policies include provisions that indicate that by using the account you are consenting to this data collection. Furthermore, most websites now make use of a software called "Internet Cookies." You will likely notice the popup bars when you first visit a website asking you to agree to install their browser cookies. Cookies track your activity on the website (what pages you visit, how long you spend on them, the links you click, and files you download) and store this information in a file on your computer. The next time you visit the website, the site can access this information. Cookies are what cause ads for the product you searched for on Amazon to appear on other websites. Most of the time, this is done without nefarious purposes in mind. The company wants to be able to convince you to keep using their service or buying their products, and to do that they need target you specifically, so they collect information that is otherwise typically innocuous. For example, that you put a pair of jeans into your cart and waited for them to come on sale before buying is meaningless to pretty much everyone besides the company you bought them from.

The most controversial way companies can collect information is by purchasing it from data brokers. This isn't a new technique, nor is it going away any time soon. Data brokers collect anonymous data chunks of various kinds to compile vast collections of information for different markets and purposes. They then sell that data to corporations looking to expand their own databases for marketing research. The kinds of data are endless, but to give you an idea, here are some examples:

- *Consumer profiles*: Data brokers will use software to create reports based on the information they collect. Some of these reports are consumer profiles, that is, a hypothetical consumer based on trends and averages they see in similar demographics. So, perhaps the data finds a trend that young women in college spend a lot of time watching beauty vloggers. This profile could help a makeup company target their advertising to young women in college by buying ad space or sponsorships with popular beauty vloggers.
- *Consumer trends*: Corporations don't have the time or people to dedicate to combing through online sources like blogs, Twitter, Facebook, and YouTube videos and comments to see what consumers are saying about their brand, or other brands in their market, and how they feel about certain products and practices. Instead, data brokers will find this information and compile it into summaries and conclusions for corporations to review and use to shape their future decisions.

Companies use data-driven marketing to retarget previous customers, optimize paid searches (i.e. Google top results), target email campaigns, and engage in dynamic advertising on social media. The goal is to keep ahead of the curve and keep business good. Businesses like banks will also use data brokers to track the spending habits of certain groups to identify credit risks in loan applicants. Typically, this data is anonymous, or, if not, it will be encrypted to reduce the risk of fraud and theft. This can sound pretty invasive, and in some ways it is. As mentioned above, the issue has more to do with the concept of gathering information through what is essentially surveillance and tracking.

Unfortunately, privacy laws haven't really addressed the idea of data brokers and implicit data. This is because the explicit data is removed from the information, therefore eliminating the possibility for someone to identify an individual in the data set. But data mining and profiling isn't all bad. For example, profiling is how credit card companies flag potential fraudulent purchases. If you typically use your card at coffee shops in New York City and suddenly a purchase is made at a hardware store in Austin, Texas, the system will compare that purchase to your previous history and likely determine it is fraudulent and either automatically decline the purchase or allow it; in both cases, it will alert you to the purchase. Geo-tracking and IP monitoring is another data mining method which can help prevent fraudulent sign-ins to your accounts. Most of us have received an email telling us that an attempt was made to sign into one of our accounts in another country while we are still sitting at home or work. This allows us to change our passwords and keep data thieves away from our information. Specific regulations regarding privacy in this space will be covered in Chapter III.

Chapter II: Domestic and International Security

DOMESTIC AND INTERNATIONAL REGULATIONS

The rise of the Internet caused a huge spike in globalization. Being able to connect instantly with a person or business on the other side of the planet has meant that our small personal worlds are suddenly massive at the push of a button. The power that comes with this connection is immense, and governments all over the world are in the throes of creating legislation to deal with online issues. But this task is a difficult one, as the online landscape is constantly changing, and different groups have varying ideas on what role laws should and should not play in regulating the Internet and its content. Furthermore, while some sites and content are region locked, the Internet is primarily international and border-crossing. This means that laws and regulations have to take into consideration existing and potential rules from other countries. This is especially important to global corporations like YouTube, Google, and Facebook.

Here are some of the key American laws affecting the Internet and the exchange of information:

1. **Cybersecurity Information Sharing Act (CISA):** Passed in 2015, the CISA is intended to allow for enhanced sharing of information to identify and prevent cybersecurity threats. To do this, it allows for the creation of an information sharing system that would give ISPs and other companies with access to Internet traffic data a direct link to government security agencies. It also includes a provision to prevent the sharing of personal data that isn't directly linked to cybersecurity.

2. **Electronic Communications Privacy Act of 1986 (ECPA):** The ECPA was the original act that the FISA (from Chapter I) amended. It establishes the basic privacy rights for individuals with regard to electronic communication (phones, GPS, email, Internet history, chat rooms, etc.) and gives the government permission to wiretap electronic devices under appropriate circumstances.

3. **Computer Fraud and Abuse Act (CFAA):** The CFAA makes accessing protected or otherwise locked computers without proper authorization a crime. This applies in any case where data is accessed through inappropriate means.

4. **Children's Online Privacy Protection Act (COPPA):** Due to how easy it is to access adult or otherwise mature content online, the COPPA specifically regulates content geared toward children (13 years old and younger). It requires that sites for children must comply with the Federal Trade Commission's (FTC) guidelines surrounding content, language, advertising, and information collection.

This list is by no means comprehensive, as we've already touched on some legislation in previous sections. For the laws surrounding Net Neutrality specifically, see Chapter V. We will look at censorship, intellectual property, more detailed privacy legislation, and free speech in Chapter III. For now, let's look at some legislation in other countries that currently affect the global Internet market.

An interesting fact to consider is that there is currently no major cybersecurity treaty existing between countries. Instead, countries solve international cyber disputes on a case-by-case basis using existing national and international laws. Given the rate at which technology changes, this method may soon be inadequate to tackle these problems, but for now it's all that we've got. Establishing a global treaty will also be especially difficult given the variety of approaches each country has to cybersecurity. Despite this, there is a group of countries so-called the "Five Eyes" which tend to be the most in contact regarding digital intelligence sharing: the U.S., U.K., Australia, New Zealand, and Canada.

In Canada, the foremost group responsible for cybersecurity is the Communications Security Establishment (CSE) which is overseen by the Department of National Defence. They are responsible for maintaining cybersecurity of critical systems and servers for the federal government, as well as monitoring cyberspace for potential threats from domestic and foreign entities. Under the National Defence Act, the CSE's purposes are to "acquire and use information from the global information infrastructure [the Internet, primarily] for the purpose of providing foreign intelligence," "provide advice, guidance and services to help ensure the protection of electronic information and information infrastructures of importance to the Government of Canada," and "to provide technical and operation assistance to federal law enforcement and security agencies in the performance of their lawful duties." They focus primarily on foreign intelligence and say they only investigate Canadians who are known associates of persons of interest. Otherwise, they comply with the Privacy Act, Anti-Terrorism Act, and the Canadian Charter of Rights and Freedoms. A bill currently working its way through congress would give the CSE expanded authority to take action against cyber threats to Canadian systems by granting them more autonomy to act without higher approval and to act sooner when a threat is detected. The Personal Information Protection and Electronic Documents Act (PIPEDA) has also been expanded to include a breach notification provision that requires organizations subject to PIPEDA to report significant breaches to the Privacy Commissioner as well as the individuals affected. Failure to do so could result in a fine from C$10,000 up to C$100,000. However, the PIPEDA only applies to Canadian private sector organizations. The Payment Card Industry Data Security Standard (PCI DSS), however, applies to all companies that accept, process, store, or transmit credit card information. They are required to pass quarterly scans conducted by Visa or MasterCard to check for vulnerabilities in security, as well as complete self-assessments on their digital security measures.

The European Union recently introduced an aggressive bill called General Data Protection Regulation (GDPR). While it has the most effect on users in the EU, it affects any company that gathers information on a citizen in the EU. This means YouTube, Facebook, Netflix, Instagram, and Snapchat, etc. must all comply with the GDPR for their operations in the EU. The first requirement is that data collection must be done with explicit and informed consent, so terms and conditions have to be easily understood and more boxes have to be checked by the user to certify they understand. Users in the EU now also have a right to revoke consent at any time and they can request the company provide a copy of any data collected. The GDPR also has more specific rules on how companies can share the collected data. Finally, the legislation affects breach reporting and mandates that companies inform authorities of breaches within 72 hours of discovering them and then users "without undue delay." Companies who do not comply with the GDPR face a fine of up to €20 million ($26 million U.S.) or four percent of their global annual revenue, whichever is higher. It's a steep penalty, so companies will have to think carefully about how they do business online in the EU and how they protect any information they collect there.

Australia recently passed a series of laws that give law enforcement agencies permissions similar to those given in the U.S. by FISA when it comes to investigating suspected terrorist activities. These laws have international consequences as well, as they now give the government the power to compel companies like WhatsApp and Facebook to cooperate with investigations through concealing covert law enforcement operations or giving them access to devices and records. Supporters of the legislation say it will allow police and agents to proceed with more safety and assurance since they can more easily obtain intelligence before an operation, thus leading to more successful terror intervention. Opponents believe that the law sets a terrifying precedent and could lead to abuses of privacy rights. Google and Twitter opposed the law because it will require them to create vulnerabilities in their systems which could in turn be exploited later. You may recall the case between Apple and the FBI in 2016. Tim Cook refused to allow his employees to create a program that could break iPhone security measures to help the FBI in its case against one of the two shooters in the San Bernardino attack. He was worried that the precedent, and software, would be used by bad actors in the future. Had this case taken place in Australia, these new laws could have been employed to force Apple to comply. Interestingly, Australia has no general constitution or charter of human rights, so the right to privacy is not one recognized by Australian law. Instead, they have a Privacy Act, which some see as inadequate in the current digital climate and given these new terror laws.

As for New Zealand, they introduced the Cyber Security Strategy and Action Plan in 2015 and have recently proposed an update to it to reflect new advancements in technology and digital culture. New Zealand's National Cyber Security Center (NCSC) published in the *Cyber Threat Report 2016-17* that of the 396 cybersecurity incidents in that 12-month period, they were able to intervene in 31 cases. They also reported "an upward trajectory of cybersecurity threats." While this update is still in its drafting stages, the goals align with the other nations discussed here, with everyone acknowledging the transnational impact of cybercrime and the need for collaboration in fighting it.

COLLECTION AND USE OF PERSONAL DATA: NATIONAL SECURITY

In Chapter I, we looked at government surveillance and some of the ways in which the government typically collects and uses personal data. For this section, we will look at how the NSA and other organizations interact with the legislation we discussed. The main section in the Foreign Intelligence and Surveillance Act most relevant to our discussion is 215, which is the part that requires phone carriers and ISPs to keep records of communications made with their services.

Phone records and Internet browsing history are the most collected kinds of personal data. The collection starts with the service providers who keep records of who contacted who, who searched for what term and visited what websites, and when. They can't just access this information for fun, though. These records are only accessible with warrants from the National Security Agency. Remember, the Foreign Intelligence Surveillance Act and Privacy Act protect your personal data from being invaded unlawfully by individuals, companies, and even the government. In order to get access to a set of records, the NSA must demonstrate probable cause to the Foreign Intelligence Surveillance Court. If they can reasonably prove that the suspicion of the target is justified, they will obtain a warrant to have the phone company or ISP turn over any records they have on that subject and their associates.

As one might assume from the Court in charge of the process and the act these warrants are made under, these requests have to be related to national security and major acts of terrorism, not just general criminal activity. Some other government agencies have argued that they should also have access to this data, not just the NSA. This would give permission to agencies who investigate crimes like drug trafficking and money laundering to apply for warrants to help in their investigations as well. So far, these requests have been denied and widely opposed because of how many people's data would potentially be available. The NSA will occasionally share their information with groups other than the FBI and CIA (who are among the main players in national security), but this is only in cases of national security. The Drug Enforcement Agency (DEA) experienced a scandal in 2013 when Reuters reported that they were secretly using tips from this highly sensitive NSA data to initiate or forward regular criminal investigations and then covering it up by reverse engineering the chain of evidence and discovery to make it look legitimate. It should be noted that according to the Privacy and Civil Liberties Oversight Board, there has never been a coordinated and intentional misuse of this data collection service. The individuals in the DEA acted outside of the law and thus acted in bad faith even though their intentions were good in wanting to stop more criminals.

Returning to the present—in 2017, the government was granted access to the phone records of 40 people, plus their associates. Interestingly, the number of people under active surveillance went down from 1,687 wiretaps in 2016 to 1,337 in 2017. The population of the United States in that same year, 2017, was 325.7 million, meaning that 0.00041% of Americans were under surveillance. That doesn't mean there aren't still opponents to Section 215. These opponents argue that any passive data collection equates to ethical misconduct and opens the door to misuse. There are also the requisite conspiracy theorists, as well, who claim the government is lying about how much data they collect and how often they analyze it. Due to the nature of their business, the NSA, FBI, and CIA are highly confidential agencies, so they are unable to provide concrete information to address some of the concerns. They have, however, declassified several successful missions and initiatives since whistle-blower Edward Snowden brought the public's attention to FISA and the Patriot Act in 2013, prompting people to demand proof that this surveillance was worth it. In 2013, former FBI director Sean Joyce testified that "over 50" potential terrorist plots were discovered and prevented since the program's beginning after the September 11 attacks. The NSA also reports that Section 702 has led to the prevention of $1 million of weapons from falling into the hands of terrorist groups in the Middle East, helped a European nation stop an aspiring terrorist from committing an attack on their soil, and they were able to learn details about a foreign military system that would allow them to have an advantage at countering it if it was used against the U.S.

In early March of 2019, a Republican congressional aide named Luke Murry went on a podcast called Lawfare and mentioned that the NSA hadn't made any requests under Section 215 in several months. Section 215 is set to expire at the end of 2019, so this new information suggests that the collection of phone metadata will likely stop at the end of the year, though the NSA has neither confirmed nor denied this claim. They still have other methods for gathering data on U.S. citizens for the purposes of national security, however, this just means the most contentious one is potentially going away at the stroke of midnight January 1, 2020.

HACKING AND COUNTER HACKING

When many of us hear the word "hacker," we tend to think of a white man in his early 30s who is either overweight or noticeably skinny, has glasses, and is sitting in a dark room in front of a series of computer monitors full of indecipherable code and 24-hour news feeds, and for some reason everything is tinted just a little bit green. This is how hackers are typically portrayed in movies and TV shows, as computer nerds who like to cause varying degrees of trouble in digital spaces. In the early days of computing, the people who would identify as hackers were nothing like this modern stereotype and were instead considered enthusiasts just trying to test the limits of computer systems. Not to cause trouble or do damage, but to find vulnerabilities so they could be fixed and to simply see how the systems worked in different circumstances.

Something these original hackers have in common with modern ones is that they tend to see computers as flawed systems in need of examination and improvement. Hacker in itself is not a negative title, and the word originally described computer enthusiasts. In fact, many hackers tend to abide by a set of three principles in their pursuits. Here they are as outlined by computing professor and researcher Herman T. Tavani:

1. Information should be free.
2. Hackers provide society with a useful and important service.
3. Activities in cyberspace are virtual in nature and thus do not harm real people in the real (physical) world.

It is obviously not possible for all information to be free as that would deny people the right to privacy as well as cause issues in national and international security. Critics call this type of thinking idealistic and even naïve, but the counter argument is that not all information has to be free. Hackers tend to believe that a lot of the information that is private should actually be free, and some information that is free, could actually be made private. The difficulty here is, who decides the parameters for putting information into each category? Is this not already a debate being had by courts, governments, corporations, and individuals and seeing conflicting and unsatisfactory results? No one seems to have an answer.

The argument that hackers provide a service to society is based on the fact that they expose security vulnerabilities, thus prompting the appropriate parties to take action to fix them. Much like the first principle, though, this is a flawed argument because we would not similarly claim that an arsonist exposing a faulty sprinkler system deserves thanks for setting a fire, nor does an underage teen reveal the flaws with IDs when he successfully buys alcohol with a fake one. Regardless, non-malicious hacking has proven helpful since its inception. For example, hackers discovered that Sony was secretly spying on users' computers through a spyware installed on their music CDs. Many hackers have also been employed by large companies and paid to break into various parts of their networks and then help with fixing the problem so it can't be exploited by bad actors later.

Finally, the claim that virtual damage does not equate to real world damage is possibly the hardest one to try and justify. Perhaps this could be argued back when computers were merely a tool used for data storage and word processing, but now that our lives are so inextricably digital, any harm done via virtual means can have real world consequences. To prove that, we need look no further than cyberbullying, where in some cases people were actually driven to suicide because of the hateful treatment they received online. Once again, though, non-malicious hackers assert that because their hacking is done in a vacuum with good intentions, they are actually preventing real world harm through their virtual actions.

Now that we have explored a little bit about "ethical," or non-malicious, hackers, let's examine the act of hacking and whether hacking and counter hacking can ever be considered ethical or right.

When it comes to cybersecurity, there are three main kinds of attacks: access to restricted data, attacks on system resources (such as an operating system) via malicious software, and attacks on networks (internal and public alike). Data security deals with unauthorized access to protected data such as personal files, employee records, and confidential information. System security refers to protecting a system's hardware, operating system software, and applications. It is thus concerned with viruses, malware, worms, and other such malicious software. Finally, network security is all about keeping internal and public networks (like the Internet) operational and safe from bad actors. Network attacks can result in data breaches, surveillance and hijacking, or the complete disabling of network access and activity.

Ethics in cybersecurity is often about how to protect users from having their rights to privacy and autonomy violated. We know that it is wrong to steal someone's information for purposes of fraud because fraud infringes on a person's right to autonomy. This is also the case with mass, unwarranted surveillance. Similarly, our devices are extensions of ourselves and are our property, therefore, intrusion into and damage of these devices constitutes a violation of rights in the same way breaking and entering or vandalism do.

Counter hacking, also referred to as active defense hacking, is a moral and legal gray area in cybersecurity. It is the act of engaging in hacker activities to either prevent an attack or to attack back. This can be done through active defense which would be a real-time response via malware or spyware that is sent to the intruder's device during the attack. Or it could involve a counter hack later on with the intention of retrieving stolen data and deleting it from the attacker's storage. As it currently stands in the United States, most forms of hacking are made illegal under the Computer Fraud and Abuse Act and the Justice Department advises against counter hacking in its cyber-crime manual.

While it seems like an appropriate response to unauthorized digital invasions and theft, counter hacking can also cause collateral damage because of the methods by which hackers get in in the first place. Many hacking programs use IP spoofing to avoid detection and make it harder for law enforcement to find them. IP spoofing is the act of hijacking another person's device IP address and using it as a cloak over your own. As a result, any real-time response triggered by a breach, such as the malware mentioned above, would affect the innocent device before it reached the origin point, if it did at all. Opponents of counter hacking argue that it is just a form of vigilantism and amounts to taking the law into one's own hands using the logic of "two wrongs make a right."

In 2017, Representative Tom Graves proposed the Active Cyber Defense Certainty Act (ACDC, reference to the rock band likely unintentional). Some referred to it as a "stand your ground law for cyberspace." In it, Graves sought to outline a series of circumstances in which counter hacking would be a legally permissible course of action and to define the appropriate limits to that response. Most security experts were against it though, claiming it did too much to encourage wanton vigilantism and could be easily misrepresented in court by a clever lawyer. In August of 2018, Rep. Graves brought a new draft forward, but there has been no movement on it since. Until a case of hacking responded to with counter hacking is tried in court, there will likely not be any legislative movement one way or the other on the issue.

INFORMATION WARFARE

It can be difficult at first glance to distinguish between information warfare and cyberterrorism. Both use digital means to upend the status quo and successfully achieve an objective at the expense of an adversary. However, cyberterrorism is specifically referring to the use of technology and cyberspace to commit acts of terror, in or out of the digital world, whereas information warfare is the broader term for using information and technology in a combative or defensive way that isn't related to terrorism.

Information warfare can be both offensive and defensive. When a mission is taking the initiative, it is sometimes referred to as an *offensive cyberspace operation* (OCO). OCO can take the form of gathering tactical information (often via interception and decryption of confidential foreign communications), the dissemination of propaganda, or disinformation for the purposes of demoralization or manipulation. An entity may also interfere with television, Internet, and radio transmissions by hijacking or jamming them. Defensive information operations may be more passive intelligence analyses using methods such as social media monitoring, or the active prevention of cyberwarfare by an adversary.

However, information warfare isn't entirely new. The U.S. Air Force had Information Warfare Squadrons as early as the 1980s. They even changed their mission to "To fly, fight and win…in air, space, and cyberspace" to reference the importance of information warfare in modern theaters of war. Even earlier still, during World War Two, one of the only ways to communicate long distance was by radio, but this method was sorely inadequate as the enemy could listen in and break through the existing encryption methods easily. Until SIGSALY, that is. SIGSALY was a speech encipherment system that was enormous (spanning 2,000 square feet) and had to be operated in a certain temperature range because there was so much sensitive equipment involved. It also required an entire division of engineers to operate, as well as a team to manage the calls themselves. SIGSALY machines allowed the allied leaders, such as Churchill and Roosevelt, to communicate with guaranteed secrecy and facilitated an estimated 3,000 encrypted communications. The system was nicknamed "The Green Hornet" after a radio show from the 1940s that had a buzzing theme song because anyone who tried to listen to an encrypted message would only hear buzzing. This use of technology was an early method of defensive information warfare. It allowed the allied leaders to pass information in secret in order to gain advantage over the axis powers and was key to winning the war.

War is devastating, but humans seem no closer to ending its practice, and its longevity has spawned an entire focus of debate called *just war theory* or *jus bellum justum* in the original Latin. Just war theory refers to the set of general understandings and criteria that humans have explicitly or implicitly agreed are the "ethical standards" for wars.

This is a fascinating juxtaposition many will dismiss as an oxymoron, while others defend it as a way of regulating something that is unlikely to be eliminated any time soon. There are a number of perspectives on just war theory from various religious doctrines to historical traditions, as well as modern directives from organizations such as the United Nations (UN). Just war theory is how we determine what constitutes a war crime and what is simply an unfortunate part of war. The two main principles in *jus in bello* ("the law in waging war") are discrimination and proportionality. Discrimination means targeting only military institutions and not illegitimate targets like civilians and neutral parties. Proportionality is the justifiably warranted amount of force to be used in operations.

Just war theory in the Information Age is complicated by the new ways to engage in information warfare. OCO are far easier to engage in than traditional military operations and could violate both guiding principles of *jus in bello*. Due to the interconnected nature of cyberspace, OCO have a chance of interfering with unintentional targets, which would go against proper discrimination and could result in unintended consequences that break proportionality expectations. Many military and legal experts agree that the rules and laws governing cyberwarfare are woefully inadequate and insist that there needs to be a codified set of guidelines to regulate war in the digital realm.

However, countries are having trouble agreeing on accepted principles with the major players in cyberwarfare (U.S., Russia, the U.K., and China) often having drastically opposing views on the specifics. This is despite everyone generally agreeing that establishing appropriate norms for behavior in cyberspace should be a priority. Russia and the U.S. seem to have agreed that OCO should follow the same rules as jus in bello, in that they should avoid directly harming civilians and civilian infrastructure, target legitimate military installations with the intention of minimizing collateral damage, and are comparable to physical attacks using the rule of proportionality. In 2015, the U.S. also spearheaded a movement to have members of the UN agree to a set of cyber rules for peacetime: no interfering with critical infrastructure, no interfering with computer emergency response teams, to assist and cooperate with investigations of cyberattacks, and to accept responsibility for attacks originating in their state. Unfortunately, due to a number of obstructionist states, among which are likely China and Russia, opposing key components to the agreement, further talks came to a halt in 2017. Some participants in the discussions claimed that cyberspace and cyberwarfare are too new to fully grasp their implications and having more talks would be premature. They argued that setting specific rules for information warfare in the digital space, including those for countermeasures and retaliation, would send states the wrong message and could be seen as permission to engage in these activities, thus undermining the call for peaceful conflict resolution and cooperation.

In 2013, the UN agreed that international law and the UN Charter should also apply to activities in cyberspace. However, China has routinely said it does not agree with the application of international law to cyberspace, stating that the Charter is sufficient. This was another of the sticking points for the 2017 report discussed above. The UN Charter states in Article 2.4 that members should avoid threats and use of force against the "territorial integrity or political independence of any state." But in Article 51, it also concedes that countries should, and do, have the right to defend themselves against such threats or uses of force, within reason. If these rules also applied to cyberspace, the difficulty would lie in determining what constituted a threat and what the appropriate response would be. In physical space, marching a battalion or sailing a fleet to another nation's borders without notice is quite clearly a threat. Borders in cyberspace are more difficult to define and threats, as defined by the UN Charter, are not as easy to identify and categorize.

There has been a steady rise in cyber information warfare in the last two decades, so the world will eventually have to address the issue. Until then, it is up to individual nations to craft their own ethical and legal code for operations in cyberspace. For now, we will move on to cyberterrorism committed by non-state-sponsored operators.

CYBERTERRORISM

Cyberterrorism is typically understood as an act committed via the Internet with the intention of achieving some political or ideological goal. The result of all terrorism is mass panic and fear, which results in the destabilization of a society, thus making it easier for the terrorist, or terrorist group, to accomplish their larger goal. Cyberterrorism is different from typical terrorism because it does not necessarily involve any physical harm to people or buildings. Instead, the perpetrators may cause exclusively digital harm in order to evoke panic and chaos. They can do this with computer viruses, worms, or widespread phishing scams. Some experts claim that cyberterrorism does not exist and is instead a form of cybercrime or information warfare. We will look at both sides of the argument in this section as we address the difficulty of defining cyberterrorism and how that affects classifying certain activities as such.

The current generally acknowledged definition for cyberterrorism is that it is any attack using computer technology or the Internet which is inspired by a political, religious, or ideological cause, intended to scare or intimidate a government or public, and interferes with infrastructure. If the act is committed in any other context, it is more likely to be regarded as cybercrime (see Chapter III), or cyberwarfare if it is conducted by a government (see previous section). Opponents to the cyberterrorism label believe that due to the lack of physical harm, these activities cannot be considered terrorism. They say that current technology, as well as current protective measures, would not allow a cyberattack to cause the kind of damage required to result in mass terror and significant loss of life. Let's look at two cyberattacks and compare them against these parameters.

In 2010, a disgruntled Australian man hacked into the waste management system in Maroochy Shire, Queensland and released raw sewage into local parks and rivers. While nobody was hurt, the result was a horrible stench for people living in the area and massive damage to the local ecosystem. He was apparently motivated by having had his job application turned down by the area's Council. The reason for the attack was related to the Council and their decision, but not necessarily political, and it seems like he wanted to cause some havoc as revenge. While definitely inconvenient and harmful to the local wildlife, this attack doesn't really fit our definition of cyberterrorism. Instead, this would be a cybercrime involving hacking and system sabotage.

In 2017, computers across the globe were infected by the WannaCry ransomware virus. It spread quickly and cost the world approximately $4 billion, all told. Luckily, a security researcher found out how to disable it and spread the word about the fairly simple kill switch. U.S. Homeland Security investigated and reported that there is reason to believe North Korean agents with potential ties to the government were behind the attack, but that hasn't been proven beyond a reasonable doubt. Because the perpetrators were never caught, it's hard to say exactly what the motive was beyond blackmail. However, it clearly interfered with infrastructure when it infected six hospitals in the U.K., causing them to have to shut down while the ransomware was dealt with. Furthermore, the attack had a global impact over the course of a day and reignited worldwide worry over cyberattacks. Yet, despite all that, few outlets referred to this attack as cyberterrorism.

Some theories suggest that this hesitation is due to the lack of examples of cyberattacks of this scale. The sample size simply isn't big enough for people to effectively categorize each event, let alone call it cyberterrorism when we are so used to terrorism involving violence and mass loss of life. But this may not always be the case as technology continues to improve and be integrated into our lives.

"Terrorism" and "terrorist" seem to be ever-present terms in our collective consciousness in the 21st century. All discussions of terrorism should address the potential for hyperbole, or overexaggerating of facts, by the media and other groups. We look at this in depth in Chapter V, but for now it's important to understand that the 24-hour news cycle and the prevalence of emotionally-charged propaganda can end up callously using a terrorist attack as a political or ideological talking point or misusing the classification of "terrorism" and causing people to be overly paranoid. This obsession with terrorism results in the media being oversaturated with sensationalized terrorist coverage and tends to lead to catastrophizing. The human brain is much more easily persuaded by emotion and story than it is by logic and statistics, so when we see a lot of coverage on terrorism, we immediately think that we are likely to be at risk even though the facts say otherwise.

This doesn't seem like a problem on the surface because perceiving a threat means you are more likely to seek out protective measures, right? Unfortunately, that's not what happens. When we overestimate a potential threat, we actually tend to overreact and make decisions that seem like they're helping when they're really just reactionary and baseless. But because we think we're safer, we feel safer, and we can end up justifying a lot of unnecessary "security measures." This is referred to as *security theater*. Some examples of security theater that many of us have encountered would be the requirement of taking off your shoes at the airport to go through security, or the requirement of a signature when making a credit card purchase. The problem with security theater is that they are often measures implemented in response to a major incident and have to be just as public and seemingly impactful as the tragedy or else people will claim the authorities are doing nothing to protect them. It's possible that in pursuing security theater, we actually divert resources from real solutions and prevention methods. This doesn't mean we should stop watching the news, but it does mean we should be aware of our initial response to threats and bad news and try our best to correct for it when we explore security measures.

In the world of cyberterrorism, this matters because it is such a new threat, we don't really know what form it will take in the future. As we give computers more and more control over complex systems, we put ourselves at greater risk and have to take security measures seriously. The WannaCry software got into hospitals, banks, delivery systems, telephone companies, and more. What if the program had managed to do more than just shut down system access until a ransom was paid? Advocates for defining cyberterrorism argue that these types of questions need to be considered before they become a reality. We should anticipate the threat so we can plan our response. Others believe that considering these questions will entice the bad actors to create the malware we want to prevent. One fact remains true: so long as people are programming computers, there will be people seeking to hack into them, and some of them will have dangerous goals.

Chapter III: Legal Issues in Cyberspace

FREE SPEECH ISSUES

Issues surrounding free speech online are sensitive subjects rife with a lot of disagreement, vague legislation, contradictory precedents, and personal interpretation. Just because a topic is difficult, however, doesn't mean we shouldn't educate ourselves on it. In an effort to try and stay neutral and informative, we will look at the legal definitions of free speech, hate speech, bullying, and similar terms in our discussion. We will also look at the regulation of certain content and how the law and personal beliefs can align or be conflicted in these cases. The Internet has also generated new forms of and trends in communication, such as spam and pop-up ads, that have initially been justified under free speech but are being questioned by consumer rights groups.

The First Amendment is the article of the U.S. constitution guaranteeing citizens the right to "the freedom of speech." Under this umbrella, the text most notably includes, apart from speech, expression of religion, freedom of the press, freedom of association, and the right to peaceful assembly. Further rulings have also included the freedom from compelled speech (being required to say or pay to be able to say certain things). The freedom of speech defense does not apply in cases of obscenity (under law), defamation, and private action against free speech.

In 1957, the Supreme Court ruled in Roth v. United States that freedom of speech does not apply in cases of obscenity as defined by the obscenity laws. Initially, obscene material was determined using the Hicklin test (from Regina v. Hicklin, a British case from 1868), which defined it as material intended "to deprave or corrupt those whose minds are open to such immoral influences, and into whose hands a publication of this sort may fall." The problem with this test is that intention is hard to prove, and the definition of immoral influences has changed over time. So, the Supreme Court also outlined a new measure called the Roth test, which says that we must consider "whether to the average person, applying contemporary community standards, the dominant theme of the material, taken as a while, appeals to the prurient [salacious, indecent] interest." They further expanded on this in 1973 during Miller v. California to also include whether the content "depicts or describes, in a patently offensive way, sexual conduct specifically defined by the applicable state law" and if the content "taken as a whole, lacks serious literary, artistic, political, or scientific value." These clarifications mean that the burden of proof of obscenity claim is much more concrete now and requires that prosecutors do their due diligence and cannot easily apply biased reasoning.

The Internet has a bad reputation for triggering a pornography revolution that has challenged obscenity laws in most states. While there are many individuals and religious groups who disagree with the law, pornography is legal so long as the participants are consenting adults. In 1969, the Supreme Court said that "if the First Amendment means anything, it means that a State has no business telling a man, sitting in his own house, what books he may read or what films he may watch" even though they may prohibit or restrict the sales or mailing of obscene material. This does not, however, apply to any kind of child pornography, even computer-generated material that does not depict an actual child (so long as it is clearly intended to be a child), under the PROTECT Act of 2003.

Defamation refers to two similar but separate crimes: libel and slander. Defamatory statements are defined as false statements or misrepresentations of facts that harm a person or group's reputation and are disseminated with intended malice. Slander is a spoken action of defamation whereas libel requires the publication of the slanderous material. Similarly to when they ruled on the strength of proof needed to declare content obscene, the Supreme Court ruled in 1964 that, in cases involving public figures and/or the press, there needed to be "clear and convincing evidence" that the publication was made with "actual malice" and "knowledge that it was false or with a reckless disregard of whether it was false or not." However, in cases between private individuals, the burden of proof is less cumbersome because freedom of speech often applies due to the lack of public consequence. With regard to online actions, defamation cases are potentially made easier due to the permanent nature of things on the Internet. Thanks to the ability to save and print emails, screencap Tweets and Facebook posts, and dig up old blog posts, evidence of malicious libel may be easier to find. However, due to the breadth and reach of the Internet, the damage done by a libelous statement could be extensive. When determining the consequences and reparations for a libelous statement, courts must consider what damage is actually relevant to the reparations.

Many people believe that having the right to the freedom of speech means that no one can limit that right. This is not accurate, as the First Amendment does not actually cover private spaces. If a space is traditionally considered public, such as a park, shopping mall, or grocery store, then the law says these places are protected by the First Amendment. However, they do permit owners of these properties to impose "reasonable restrictions on expressive activity" such as restricting demonstrators from entering certain areas and banning aggressively disruptive individuals (Pruneyard Shopping Center v. Robins), or not allowing you to say "bomb" in an airport. Similarly, if you work for a company or organization that has policies over what you can say and where, the First Amendment does not protect you. Teachers, for example, are held to a high standard of conduct and posting something on your private Facebook page as a teacher can be used as grounds to fire you if that post violates your union's conduct policy.

Online, this debate is a hot one right now, as we haven't completely come to a meaningful consensus on what constitutes public versus private spaces on the Internet. Rather recently, though, the courts and general public have concluded that if a private company runs a website, forum, or other online service and you as a user agree to their terms of use, they are perfectly within their rights to restrict your rights to free speech. Section 230 of the Communication Decency Act protects online hosts from being held liable for the behavior of their users and gives them permission to create and enforce reasonable codes of conduct on their platforms. If you recall our discussion of international legislation in Chapter III, you will remember that we looked at the GDPR, a law in the EU that directly contradicts Section 230 of the CDA in the United States. Alex Jones, host of the controversial conspiracy theory podcast *InfoWars*, was banned or suspended from several large social media sites in late 2018. These included his personal and podcast accounts on Twitter and Periscope, Facebook, Apple, and YouTube. All of the companies cited repeated policy violations with regard to abusive behavior in particular. Jones disputed these shutdowns by claiming the sites were violating his right to free speech, but he was denied any legal action due to Section 230, as well as the fact that, in order to use these websites, you must agree to abide by their policies with the understanding that violating them will have consequences.

You may have noticed that in looking at what the First Amendment does not protect, hate speech was not specifically mentioned. This is because the United States is one of the few liberal (free) democracies that does not regulate hate speech as clearly as other countries do. The United States does have protections against civil liberties and can prosecute hate crimes, with some being classified using the defamation laws we looked at earlier. Where free speech no longer protects hate speech is when the line is crossed from professing one's opinions to "inciting imminent lawless action and is likely to incite or produce such action." Calling people by racial derogatory names, for example, is protected under free speech in public spaces. But calling for the mass extermination of a hated group and laying out clear plans for doing so, however, is not. This is why many sites have such robust behavior policies in place to manage the discourse between its users. Otherwise, people in the U.S. wishing to pursue cases of hate speech, online or otherwise, face an uphill battle in the legal system.

PRIVACY LEGISLATION AND INDUSTRY SELF-REGULATION

Privacy legislation refers to a series of interconnected legal concepts that are applied in a variety of contexts. They define the parameters for privacy protection, such as who is protected, when, and where. They also outline the legal steps one may take if they feel their privacy has been violated and are seeking retribution for the intrusion. Finally, privacy legislation helps specify the kinds of information that can be collected and how it can be shared. In Chapter I, we referred to this as the norms of appropriateness and distribution. For this section, we will look at some privacy legislation in more depth and see how they relate to activities online, as well as look at how commercial entities look to protect your privacy "in-house."

In Chapter II, we identified key legislation affecting the flow of information in cyberspace, most of which had to do with privacy. Since we already outlined the relevant laws in Chapter II, we will move right into looking at violations of privacy and how the legislation is applied and changing with each new case. To constitute an invasion of privacy, an action must fall under one of four categories: *intrusion of solitude, public disclosure of private facts, false light,* or *appropriation.*

Intrusion of Solitude is an intentional intrusion into one's private quarters, physical or electronic. A person's private quarters are defined as any space or property (including possessions such as phones and computers) where a reasonable person presumes to have privacy. An intrusion occurs when the perpetrator intentionally uses physical means, such as their senses or an electronic device, to gain access to a person's private affairs. This means hacking into their devices, listening in on a hushed conversation, or secretly watching or recording someone for the purposes of information gathering. To qualify as an invasion of solitude, the incident simply needs to have happened, regardless of what the perpetrator did or did not do with the information gathered. Let's say you have your Facebook set to private, so only your friends can see what you post. Are you presumed privacy in your posts here? On the one hand, some would argue you are not entitled to privacy because social media is by its very nature public space, so anything you say could be free game. However, others would say that by setting it to private, you are intentionally controlling who interacts with your posts which is basically the digital equivalent of booking a private room in a restaurant. In 2018, the Supreme Court ruled that prosecutors could compel social media companies to turn over and verify the authenticity of decidedly public content, but the moment the content is put behind the private barrier, they must obtain a warrant and prove the post would be relevant to the case. It is officially private no matter the number of friends the person has. This precedent was set in a very specific set of circumstances though and brought up questions about rights to a fair trial for both defendants and plaintiffs in cases where social media is used as evidence.

Public Disclosure of Private Facts is the sharing of personal information that is truthful which most reasonable people would consider to be an objectionable action. This one is pretty straightforward and is learned by most middle-schoolers at some point when their best friend reveals a secret of theirs to one or more people without permission. The only difference is that this intermediary obtained the information through snooping rather than being explicitly told the information. Public disclosure could result in the harm of a person's reputation, their personal relationships, or even their employment opportunities. Online, there is a specific crime associated with public disclosure called *doxing*. When a hacker doxes a person, it means they have obtained their private information such as telephone numbers and home addresses for a person and their family or friends and then published it to the Internet, typically for the purposes of inciting harassment. Doxing is especially common against public figures but can happen to anyone who says something controversial and goes viral for it. Doxing is often a response in outrage culture, which we looked at back in Chapter I.

False Light is the sharing of false (though not necessarily defamatory, see Chapter V) facts which cause others to view a person in a false light. This is a hard case to adjudicate because it needs to balance the plaintiff's rights to privacy with the defendant's right to free speech. To qualify, a statement must be published in some way, be made with malicious intent, be a lie that places the defendant in a false light and be highly offensive or embarrassing. The burden of proof for false light claims is also a little lighter than libel and slander accusations because the statement made can be false *or* a misleading representation of the truth, but as a result, more decision-making power is given to the court. The other way false light differs from defamation cases is that false light is primarily concerned with protecting "the plaintiff's mental or emotional well-being" rather than their wider reputation. An example case from 1984 helps highlight these differences.

An entertainer named Jeannie Braun performed an act in an amusement park that involved swimming with a pig. A man named Larry Flynt obtained a picture of Braun with the pig and published it in a magazine devoted to showcasing lewd pictures of women, often involving animals. The result was the implication that Braun had engaged in sexual acts with the pig, which was entirely false. She sued Flynt for both defamation and false light charges and a jury awarded her settlements for both. The Fifth Circuit Court of Appeals, however, ruled that she could not receive both payments because they were for the same publication. They suggested that she waived her defamation claim because the courts would be more likely to approve the settlement under false light charges due to the "personal humiliation, embarrassment, pain and suffering" she experienced from the incident.

Appropriation is using a person's name or likeness without permission to acquire some sort of benefit. This is different from fraud because in appropriation, the perpetrator is not impersonating the individual, but rather using their likeness without consent, often for commercial purposes. An example would be someone using a photo of you and your partner announcing your new engagement to advertise their jewellery business. Unless you gave this person permission to have that photo and use it in their advertising, you could file an appropriation complaint against them. Given the ease of finding names and downloading photos online, this is often how many memes get their start. Unfortunately, due to the difficulty of tracing memes back to their originators, many claims go unsettled. In 2015, a woman in South Carolina took her daughter to meet Hillary Clinton at a campaign rally. The daughter took a picture with Clinton and it was posted to the Clinton campaign's Flickr page. From there, an anonymous person took the photo and used it to make an anti-Hillary ad filled with obscene text about genital mutilation and stoning. The mother was horrified and tried everything to get the photo taken down, but it had been shared so much and sites repeatedly denied her. Eventually, a member of the Anti-Defamation League stepped in and helped legally prove that the Clinton Campaign owned the copyright of this photo, and they used this to file takedown notices (see *Intellectual Property*) against every site they could find that hosted the photo. Eventually, it was removed from just about all of them. The woman and her daughter never received any damages for their emotional suffering, but they are using the victory to help empower other people whose images have been used without permission to take action.

Industry self-regulation is nothing new but applying the standards to a digital age requires careful consideration of how the entity uses technology. Self-regulation is any process that a company engages in with regard to setting standards and policies not explicitly outlined in legislation. This means privacy policies, codes of conduct, and terms and conditions. We cover a variety of these in Chapter V, so in favour of avoiding too much repetition, we won't go into detail here. Instead, let's quickly summarize how legislation and self-regulation work together to protect your privacy. Self-regulation determines a specific industry's best practices in its daily operations to guide its actions towards ethical behavior, while legislation is the broader, external accountability measure in place to protect consumers from being taken advantage of. Ideally, industries will put reasonable practices in places where the law doesn't reach.

INTELLECTUAL PROPERTY

Intellectual property is any intangible object created by an individual or group that belongs to them according to generally accepted copyright laws and norms. Intellectual property can be a work of art such as a song or a video, a patent for an invention not yet constructed in the physical world, or even a concept for a fictional work not yet published (within reason). In the digital realm, intellectual property can also be an app, piece of software, or a website. IPs are protected under copyright and trademark laws, which outline rules for fair use, licensing, ownership, and compensation. Many countries have updated their copyright laws to try and meet the needs of digital content creators and distributors in the 21st century. As we will see, though, the laws have so far been largely unsatisfactory either in scope or practice or both. The important thing is that lawmakers and experts continue to discuss the issue and try to come up with adequate legislation that balances fair compensation for creators as well as reasonable restrictions and punishments for everyone else.

Before we get into the specific laws and some of the concerns they present, we should briefly look at the difference between a trademark and copyright. Copyright is automatically given to the author or creator of any fixed piece of work and can be legally ratified by applying to the United States Copyright Office. When you have copyright over a piece of work, you have the power to republish the work in part or in whole, sell or give licenses to others to do the same (and revoke them), and you can pursue legal action against someone if they recreate your work without your permission. Trademark, however, protects "words, names, symbols, sounds or colors that distinguish goods and services from those manufactured or sold by others and to indicate the source of the goods." So, a pizzeria called *Jim's Pizza* can register a trademark for their name and logo. This would prevent another *Jim's Pizza* from opening and using the customer confusion to generate business. Trademarks are granted by the United States Patent and Trademark Office. An easy way to remember the difference is to think of copyright as protecting *things* and trademarks as protecting *identities*.

Another key term in our discussion in this section is *public domain*; so what is it and what does it mean when something is in the public domain? The public domain is the body of creative work that is available for the public to use free of copyright protections. Furthermore, once something is in the public domain, it cannot be purchased by anyone for a new copyright term. However, if you compile a collection of public domain works, you have created a new work which can, in some cases, be copyrighted. This is a blurry line, though, because there is also a "collective works" copyright protection which means these new works are only protected if a new creative or organizational approach is taken in arranging the collection. For example, by taking a specific selection of works such as poems about the moon or paintings featuring dogs.

Copyright in the United States is outlined primarily by the Copyright Act of 1976 and its amendments, most notably the Sonny Bono Copyright Term Extension Act (SBCTEA) and the Digital Millennium Copyright Act (DMCA). The SBCTEA extended the number of years a work remains copyrighted to the life of the author plus seventy years, previously only plus fifty years. Some people nicknamed this act the Mickey Mouse Protection Act, because it was passed just in time to prevent the original Mickey Mouse design from entering public domain. Copyright terms started expiring on January 1, 2019, and new works will enter the public domain every January 1 from now on (with the original Mickey being freed in 2024). Trademarks, however, do not expire, so Disney will still own the original Mickey Mouse trademark and will likely still pursue legal action against people attempting to use his likeness for profit.

The DMCA was enacted in 1998 and makes it a crime to create and distribute devices, software, or services meant to circumvent digital rights management (DRM) technology. DRM technology is software put into a digital file that will prevent certain actions, such as copying, from being used on the file. The DMCA is also responsible for limiting liability of companies and websites when their users commit copyright infringement, which is great for hosts like YouTube. It was inspired primarily by the rise of peer-to-peer (P2P) file-sharing. P2P is an effective method for illegal file-sharing because it uses a network of computers hosting the content to send it in bits and pieces to a new location. We will look at P2P and torrenting more later in this chapter when we discuss piracy (see *Cybercrimes*). Copyright holders, especially the music recording industry, wanted to have more direct methods for having their content removed from unauthorized websites that were appropriate to the new digital era.

To do this, copyright holders must file a DMCA takedown notice. While there is no official form to use for issuing a takedown notice, copyright holders must make written notice via letter or email. The notice should include basic contact details for the copyright holder, a URL link to the location of the original copyrighted content, any URL links to the places the infringer is hosting the stolen content, as well as the title of the content. The copyright holder must also state that the notice is being filed in good faith, the information provided is accurate, and that they have legal right to make this claim as they are the copyright holder or are authorized to act on their behalf.

Once a notice is filed, the content host must either remove the infringing content or counter the notice by presenting a valid license to use the copyrighted content or claim it under fair use (discussed below). While webhosts are typically protected from liability if their users post infringed content, they can still face penalties if they don't take copyright claims seriously. They can be found guilty by association for negligence or of encouraging the infringement. This is why YouTube takes the steps it does to curb copyright infringement. YouTube has a copyright complaint form for users to fill out when they discover copyright infringing material. Larger organizations that own the rights to a large body of content, such as publishers, media agents, and record labels, can apply for access to the Content ID system.

Content ID is an automatic process that scans uploaded videos for matches to their database of copyrighted materials as submitted by the copyright owners. When a match is made, both the infringing channel and the copyright holder are notified of the Content ID claim. What happens to the video depends on how the copyright holder chooses to approach the infringement. They can block videos that include their content, which results in them immediately being taken down and in their place a notice will be displayed with the reason for the takedown and the copyright holder's name. They may choose to monetize the video instead, thus receiving profits from any ads run on it. This revenue can be shared with the uploader or not. Finally, the copyright holder may choose to do nothing but get access to the viewership statistics on the video. In all of these cases, the channel has the option to dispute this claim. Sometimes content that falls into fair use will still be flagged by the Content ID system as it isn't perfect. This caused some unrest among creators on YouTube when it was first implemented because it was initially unclear what happened to the ad revenue from a video during the dispute process. YouTube has since clarified that if a channel disputes a claim within five days of the strike, YouTube will withhold all of the profits from the moment the claim was made and release them to the appropriate party when the dispute is resolved. If the dispute is made after the five-day mark, revenue will only be withheld from the day the dispute is made and any revenues paid out before that are irretrievable.

Back in 2011, two highly controversial digital copyright laws were proposed: the Stop Online Piracy Act (SOPA) and the PROTECT IP Act (PIPA). PIPA and SOPA sought to do two main things: 1) Give the government permission to have ISPs block access to copyright infringing domains even if those domains aren't in the U.S., and sue search engines, directories, blogs, and forums to have links to these blocked domains removed, and 2) Give corporations and the government the power to cut off funds to infringing websites by compelling U.S. advertisers to cancel their accounts. At first glance, this sounds perfectly reasonable. Blocking piracy sites and cutting off any revenue streams is a good thing. The problem lay more with the vague wording of the bill that would have opened the door for corporations to potentially abuse this power and cripple new web start-ups relying on user-based content. Remember, this was before the big Google and Facebook duopoly dug in its heels, so there were more search engines and social media websites for people to choose from. If these websites couldn't keep up with the required copyright monitoring, they could easily be sued into bankruptcy. These two bills would also have resulted in any copyright infringement being punishable by up to five years in prison, even if the content was a video of your dog chasing its tail to a piece of copyrighted music, and removed the host protections provided by the DMCA. Both SOPA and PIPA were subsequently shelved in 2012 after widespread disapproval.

Fair use is regulated under Section 107 of the U.S. Copyright Act. It outlines that copyrighted materials may be used without permission when it is used for criticism, commentary, news reporting, teaching, scholarship, and research. A good way to think about it is to consider fair use a transformative exercise which takes the original material and uses it in something new and different. Of course, this does not apply in all cases. For example, reproducing an entire work for criticism purposes would likely not fall under fair use while only using parts of it likely would. A number of university and legal scholar websites have "Fair Use Checklists" that a person can consult to determine ahead of time if their work will be likely to qualify under fair use. The U.S. Copyright Office uses the following criteria in determining fair use (as per their website):

1. Purpose and character of the use, including whether the use is of a commercial nature or is for nonprofit educational purposes.
2. Nature of the copyrighted work. [referring to factors such as the copyrighted work's form being creative or factual and whether it is published or not]
3. Amount and substantiality of the portion used in relation to the copyrighted work as a whole.
4. Effect of the use upon the potential market for or value of the copyrighted work.

In an effort to continue taking action against some of the biggest problems online, the European Union introduced the European Union Copyright Directive (EUCD), aimed at enforcing proper compensation for copyright holders. The EUCD hasn't yet passed into law due to vast disapproval ratings from voters and disagreement over specific articles by governing bodies. Most notably, people oppose Articles 11 and 13. Article 11 has been dubbed "The Link Tax" because it would prohibit links from displaying headlines and the first few lines of content that is shared without a copyright license or else face a fine. Article 13 "The Upload Filter," however, is far more controversial, as it requires any "online content sharing service provider" (such as YouTube, Vimeo, Twitch, or even Facebook in some cases) to "obtain an authorisation from the rightholders…for instance by concluding a licensing agreement, in order to communicate or make available to the public works or other subject matter." So, the first issue with Article 13 is that users would have to sign a contract with the website to give them permission to host the content. It also shifts the responsibility for monitoring copyrighted material from rightholders to the service itself. Unfortunately, monitoring the amount of content that is uploaded to YouTube alone would be a nearly impossible task, even if you used a combined workforce of computer ID software and real people. This may sound familiar because it is a lot like PIPA, which thankfully failed. The final vote for the EUCD is scheduled to take place on March 25, 2019.

LAWFUL ACCESS AND ENCRYPTION

In Chapter I, we briefly mentioned encryption in our overview of digital security methods. Encryption is the process of scrambling data to make it so that only those with the encryption key, or cipher, are able to unlock the data to access it. There are three main kinds of encryption: symmetric, asymmetric, and end-to-end. *Symmetric* encryption is when the same encryption key is used by all devices accessing the encrypted data. The difficulty with this kind of encryption is that the key can become compromised if it is intercepted during the initial transfer of data. However, it is perfectly fine for low stakes data like day-to-day text messages, for example. *Asymmetric* encryption involves the creation of a public key and a private key. The public key is the one that can be intercepted by a third party, but it will be useless to them without one of the private keys because you need one of each, public and private, to decrypt the data. *End-to-end* encryption is a form of asymmetric encryption and works by encrypting the data so that not even the server hosting the data can read it. This is the kind of encryption used by WhatsApp, Facebook Messenger, iMessage, and any website using Transport Layer Security (TLS) software. You can tell this is in place by the "s" at the end of https:// before the website URL. If there is no "s," they are not using TLS to help protect your data.

Encryption is one of the most reliable ways to protect your digital information because there are a practically infinite number of encryption algorithms and breaking them is incredibly difficult. So difficult that many bad actors won't bother, though this isn't always the case as we will see in the next section on cybercrime. Encryption has also become a controversial topic with regard to law enforcement, and national security in particular. Apple and Google, two of the biggest players in the tech industry, are constantly improving their encryption methods to protect users' data in cyberspace. In 2014, then FBI director James Comey publicly criticized the tech giants for this because some of their methods directly hindered law enforcement officials from accessing devices even when they had a search warrant. Apple's iOS 8 was the first of their operating systems to be so well encrypted even Apple programmers weren't able to access a locked device. Recall our discussion of the battle between Apple and the FBI in Chapter II when they refused to create a master key to unlock the phone of a suspect from the San Bernardino shootings.

This battle between law enforcement and tech companies boils down to concerns over lawful access. Many countries, especially the Five Eyes (see Chapter II), are attempting to update the digital legislation to create more specific parameters for accessing encrypted data in criminal investigations. As it currently stands, most privacy legislation prevents law enforcement from accessing any encrypted data because they are barred from hacking in the same way bad actors are. Groups advocating for these new provisions say that privacy should be protected but those security methods should be null and void when the person is suspected of a crime. Groups who oppose these provisions call them backdoors that could lead to abuse by corrupt or biased officials. A bipartisan bill was introduced in 2018 to prevent the government from granting law enforcement agencies permission to create these backdoors, called the Secure Data Act of 2018. It is currently awaiting review by the Subcommittee on Crime, Terrorism, Homeland Security, and Investigations before it returns to the House for further discussion.

CYBERCRIMES

Cybercrimes are, quite simply, crimes committed via digital means. These crimes can be a one-off incident or an ongoing scam or enterprise. There are a wide range of cybercrimes, from the mostly innocuous, such as piracy, to the malicious, such as malware and DDoS attacks. For this section we will outline a number of cybercrimes and how they are committed, as well as how you can protect yourself from bad actors in cyberspace.

Perhaps the most common cybercrime is *piracy*. Piracy is the act of obtaining copyrighted material, often for free, from an unauthorized source. The most commonly pirated materials are television shows, movies, and music, followed by software. Piracy is committed by illegally recording a piece of media, either physically or digitally, and distributing it online, and downloading or accessing pirated content uploaded by others. Any time you watch an unauthorized stream of your favorite television show, you are technically engaging in piracy. However, this sits in a moral gray area, as we discussed in Chapter I when we looked at individual conduct in cyberspace. Another kind of piracy is referred to as *cracking*. Cracking is the act of downloading a piece of software for free, either through a legitimate free trial download or from a piracy website and using something called a *key generator* (keygen) to create an unlock key for the program without having to purchase a license. This was an especially common practice for earlier versions of the Adobe Creative Suite software which could run upwards of $400 retail.

To help hide the transfer of stolen material, piracy is often committed using P2P (peer-to-peer) file transfer services. On their own, P2P services are not illegal. P2P file sharing works by creating a network between computers and sharing the file transfer load among them. Rather than the entire file being stored and transferred from a single source, the download will take parts of the file from multiple sources who are uploading their portion separately. This helps alleviate pressure on system resources during a file transfer, especially if that file is being access by a large number of people at once. However, when P2P torrents are used to obtain copyrighted material, that's when it becomes illegal. But, downloading illegal torrents is risky, as it is easy for bad actors to embed trojans and other malware in the material being shared in order to infect a large number of devices. Any time you download a file, you should scan it with an anti-virus program before opening it, just to be safe.

The next most common cybercrime is fraud. Fraud, also called identity theft, is the act of pretending to be someone else in order to gain access to restricted information and accounts for various purposes. Criminals do this by either hacking into your device or accounts through brute force or malware, or by sending you phishing emails in the hopes of tricking you into giving them your passwords. Once a bad actor has this information, they can cause a lot of damage such as opening a credit card in your name and maxing it out, getting loans in your name, committing tax or health insurance fraud, stealing funds directly from your bank account, or using you as a cover for other illegal activity. Fraud is a highly destructive crime and victims will sometimes have to spend years putting their lives back together after having their identity stolen. To protect yourself from fraud, you should never give out your passwords to anyone, especially online. You should also make sure you have two-factor authentication turned on for every account that allows it. Furthermore, you shouldn't use the same password for more than one account because it makes it easier for criminals to do a lot of damage quickly.

Phishing is a scam that involves bad actors pretending to be a trusted source in order to trick you into giving them confidential information like passwords, credit card information, or bank account numbers. The name phishing was chosen because it is a homophone of fishing where people will use bait in order to catch their prey. Phishing scams can be committed over the phone but are now most commonly seen in email form. These emails will pretend to be from a bank or other company and often claim that your account has been compromised and to click a link and sign in to verify your identity. At first glance, these emails are pretty convincing, with the well-crafted ones using official-looking formats, company logos, and real employee names. However, the link will actually take you to a fake webpage that will send the information you submit right to the scammer. Luckily, email clients are constantly improving their AI to detect spam and can filter out most phishing scams, automatically sending them to your junk folder. It's still important to be aware of phishing scams, though, and to always double check sender names and email addresses. If it looks even kind of suspicious, call the company using a number from their actual website and ask customer service if the email is legitimate.

Another risk in cyberspace is malware, the shorthand for malicious software. Malware can take the form of computer viruses, trojans and keyloggers, spyware and ransomware, and more. Malware is a huge danger online because of how easily hidden it is. Malware can be installed by clinking on a link or ad or downloading a file. They can do everything from brick (kill) your device to track your usage and send your data to a third party to simply mess with your system by triggering infinite popups and changing key bindings. Earlier in this chapter we looked at the WannaCry ransomware that infected computers across the globe. Luckily, there are a number of highly effective anti-virus programs that scan your device for threats so it can isolate and destroy them before they do any damage. Much like encryption, it is just good sense to have a good anti-virus in place to protect your system. Some threats, like trojans and keyloggers, are really good at hiding and you may never notice them yourself, so it's important to have that added layer of security.

When you look at all of these cybercrimes one after another, it can make cyberspace look really dangerous, and in many ways it is. But it's no more dangerous than crossing a busy street at rush hour. If you take the proper precautions and educate yourself on potential threats, you greatly reduce your risk of being victimized. It is inevitable that you will be targeted at some point; data is being stolen and leaked all the time. But criminals face an uphill battle through the network of security measures in place online and on systems. If you arm yourself with knowledge and take potential threats seriously then you will be able to navigate the digital world safely.

Chapter IV: Technological Innovation and Ethics

BIOTECHNOLOGIES

Biotechnology is a staple of most science fiction stories, promising us advanced robotic limbs and technological conveniences like having credit card information built into a chip in our hands. Even though *Back to the Future* got the flying car prediction wrong, we are seeing plenty of research progress in areas once thought to be purely speculative, especially when it comes to biology, for humans and everything else. Technology has allowed us greater access to the mysteries of genomes. We have successfully cloned animals and created genetic databases so the average person can trace their ancestry for a moderate fee. There are people living with identity chips in their hands and NFC chips for unlocking their front door. The modern world is running at full speed into a technological future and while that is incredibly exciting, there are a lot of questions to be asked and concerns to discuss. We have to wonder: just because we *can*, does it mean we *should*? Are certain advancements and implementations inevitable? Are we culturally, socially, and physically ready for these new technologies? Let's look at some existing and emerging biotechnologies and consider some of these questions.

Biometrics refers to body measurements that make up our unique physical and behavioral characteristics. Fingerprints, palm veins, iris and retina recognition, and DNA are examples of physical characteristics in biometrics. Behavioral characteristics can be things such as your voice, walking gait, and even your typing rhythm. Since your physical characteristics are entirely unique to you, they are a reliable identifier. Because of this, they are often used in criminal investigations to determine the guilty parties. But they are also implemented in other ways, such as authentication. Most new smart phones are equipped with biometric authentication methods such as fingerprint scanning or face recognition. Disney World in Florida also uses fingerprint biometrics to make sure that people aren't sharing passes. For now, biometrics is a great tool for verifying someone's identity. But as technology improves, ethics researchers and other experts are worried about the potential for biometric information to be amassed and stored in databanks which could result in two problems: abuse by the government or other agencies in surveillance, or highly sophisticated identity theft by hackers accessing and stealing the data. They also say we need to consider questions about what kind of data would be stored, how would we consent to this collection, who would make the rules for how that data could be used, and who would be in charge of regulating biometric data collection and accountability for misuse? At this point in time, we can only speculate about the future of biometrics.

Similar to biometrics is *bioinformatics*. Bioinformatics is an interdisciplinary field because it combines computer science, mathematics, and statistics with the study of biology. This combination has allowed for the large amounts of biological data to be used in complex computer simulations, especially aiding in the field of experimental molecular biology. It has also allowed huge advances in genome sequencing and typing, also called *genomics*, and comparison because computers can index and find data at a faster rate than humans looking through paper documents. This field has led to an evolving ethical issue surrounding the collection and use of individual genetic data—at-home DNA kits. For a variety of prices, there are a number of companies who offer DNA sequencing or genome typing to everyone, though some require a doctor's order. This is called direct-to-consumer genetic testing. You provide them with a sample, typically saliva, and they will use it to look for markers for a variety of information: where your ancestors originated, what genetic diseases you are at risk of, if you have any allergies you may not be aware of, and some even purport to tell you dietary trends such as lactose tolerance and whether you are a deep sleeper.

As more people do these tests, the results become more robust because the databases grow. But, it's important to read all of the terms and conditions before you give your DNA to a company. Ancestry.com includes a provision saying by using their testing service, you are agreeing to allow them to sell your information to pharmaceutical companies. Of course, your data is anonymous, but it is your genetic code, so it is impossible to make it *completely* anonymous. Furthermore, DNA sequences are not currently protected under HIPAA, the health privacy act that protects the rest of your medical information. Another potential issue with genetic testing is that some people don't want to know what diseases they're at risk for. Huntington's disease, for example, is a genetic disorder that results in the regular decline of cognitive, emotional, and motor functions. A Huntington's disease diagnosis, or even just the confirmation of risk, can be incredibly destructive to a person's mental health. They may drastically change the way they live their life because they feel like the disease could be just around the corner. Others, however, may find peace knowing they are at risk and will be able to handle the diagnosis better if it comes. This is something each individual must consider before doing a genetic test that looks at disease risk. These tests may also affect your insurance. Your current insurer doesn't have access to this information, but if you apply for new insurance and they ask if you are at risk for any genetic diseases and you've done one of these tests, you have to disclose the results because not doing so would be committing insurance fraud.

The final biotechnology we will look at is *microchip implants*. We've been using RFID microchips in our pets for a long time to help us find them if they get lost, but now we are seeing a rise in microchip implants in humans. People are showing growing interest in having near field communication (NFC) and RFID chips implanted in their hands to allow them a quick and secure way to do things like unlock doors, open garages, log into computers and phones, and even unlock cars. Some people call this *biohacking* and believe the next stage of human evolution is direct integration with technology. Opponents to human microchips pose risks for GPS tracking and manipulation. However, these fears are based on misinformation because NFC and RFID chips have no internal power source and therefore cannot support GPS technology nor can they affect you if someone hops onto the chip's RFID signal. If this was not the case, it would be a lot easier to find missing pets.

Newer chips are being created to serve more medical functions, such as monitoring and storing data about the body's vitals. This could be used by doctors and paramedics to get a better idea of a person's condition before they were admitted to the hospital and help enhance diagnosis and treatment. Diabetics can also now get glucose-monitoring chips, so they never have to prick their fingers again. There are plenty of questions to explore as the technology expands, such as the eventual GPS-enabled chips and other more complex devices. We cannot predict every concern or advancement, but it will be up to everyone, from scientists to law makers to the average citizen, to be involved in shaping the future of biotechnologies.

INTERNET OF THINGS

The *Internet of Things* (IoT) refers to the "ability of smart objects to be connected to the Internet for the purpose of transmitting and receiving data." This means phones and computers, but also smart TVs, coffee makers, smart watches, or mechanical parts that connect to the Internet to receive operating instructions. Some experts predict that the number of IoT devices will surpass 50 billion by 2020. The expectation is that eventually, every object that can be connected, will be connected, and they will be able to talk to each other. Let's briefly explore the pros and cons of this concept. Our discussion will primarily deal with the concept of *known unknowns*, which means that we know we do not have the answers to these questions but that we need to ask them. However, we will also touch on some implied *unknown unknowns*, which are concepts and questions we cannot adequately anticipate or consider given our current body of knowledge. A good way to think about unknown unknowns is to think about how humans had no idea DNA was a thing until we discovered it. It was an unknown unknown for a lot of human history. Let's engage in some thought experiments.

When all of your devices are connected, it can allow for seamless automation at home and in your day-to-day. Your morning alarm will sync with your coffee maker, so your morning brew is ready when you wake up. Your thermostat will read upcoming weather patterns and adjust automatically to maintain your preferred climate. Your self-driving car will sync with your calendar and check traffic information to calculate exactly when you need to leave and the route to take to get to your destination on time. Maybe it can even tell that there is a traffic jam up ahead due to an accident and texts or emails the relevant party for you, saying you will be late. The possibilities are practically endless, especially if city infrastructure also implemented these smart systems.

All of this digital interconnectedness also brings up major security concerns. If a bad actor manages to gain access to a less secure device in your home, could they then access your entire network and interfere with it? How will we protect these networks and their connections? Another concern is about the logistics of this smart city dream. All of these connections rely on servers and information storage. Entire companies will need to be created and dedicated to the maintenance and support of the system. As the number of IoT devices and connections grow, it also becomes more impossible to regulate data collection and privacy. The world would become a maze of consent forms and privacy scandals unless these concerns are anticipated as much as possible. We already looked at the difficulties surrounding privacy policies and terms and conditions, but mass connection to the IoT would make it nearly impossible for every person to give informed consent to every possible connection and use of their data. It is unreasonable to expect people to do their due diligence in thoroughly reading terms of service when they will potentially need to do so for every new store they enter and every new device they power up. People already don't typically read EULAs because they are purposefully full of complex legalese. How would we handle this change?

We may even end up in a societal panopticon. The panopticon was a prison design by Jeremy Bentham. It positioned all of the cells around a central observation tower that housed the guards. The common area was enclosed by the outer wall of cells. As a result, the inmates were under constant supervision and would supposedly behave better. However, the trick was that the windows of the central tower would allow guards to see out, but not allow inmates to see in, so they could never be sure if they were actually being watched. The control thus came more from the fear of being watched rather than actually being watched. The widespread implementation of IoT may create the same effect in society and inadvertently create a society of fear and behavioral control. This is, of course, a highly pessimistic view of technological advancement and comes with a lot of catastrophizing, but it isn't necessarily an illegitimate consideration. With current technology, this debate remains largely speculative and comes down to personal ethics and beliefs about privacy and reasonable data sharing.

ROBOTICS AND ARTIFICIAL INTELLIGENCE

Perhaps the most famous piece of science fiction that looks at ethics and robotics is *iRobot*, a collection of short stories by Isaac Asimov. In it, robots are a major part of society and are programmed to adhere to the "Three Laws of Robotics" that are specifically worded so that robots, who are bound by pure logic rather than emotion, will never harm a human and will obey all orders given to it. This is only one example of fiction that explores the ethics and concerns of robotics and artificial intelligence (AI). As real-world technology advances, this conversation is one that people are having more often now that robotics and AI are becoming a tangible reality.

There are a lot of misconceptions about robots due to popular fiction, which has led some people to not realize that robotics have already been implemented in a lot of helpful ways. Advanced prosthetic limbs, for example, are only possible because of robotics. In the past, people with prosthetic arms had very limited motor functions, but advancements in technology and biology have allowed for the development of complex robotic limbs that can use electromyography (EMG) to sense muscle movements in the remaining tissue and turn that information into the corresponding movement for the prosthetic limb. This is clearly an ethical approach to and use for robotics, but it isn't always that easy.

Perhaps the biggest concern facing robotics is automation and the consequences of that. After the industrial revolution, a lot of people found themselves out of work as machines took over simple tasks. We are facing a similar situation now as computers become more advanced and machines more sophisticated. Advocates for job security argue that lawmakers and companies need to be more involved in helping people who are declared redundant or obsolete as a result of automation with job training and transition support. They say that technological progress should not mean sacrificing moral and social responsibility. Others, however, say that it is up to the individual to make themselves competitive and invest in new skills if they can see their job is becoming obsolete; it shouldn't be on the companies to reduce profits just to save a few jobs. These are two very different ethical approaches to the same problem and is one of the reasons this discussion is so hard to bring to an actionable conclusion. Along with this is the concern over how to properly distribute the wealth accrued from automated work. With less workers to pay, companies will see more profit, but that profit will be distributed among less people. Those who are now out of work will be spending less and this could seriously harm an economy in the long run. How will we handle the transition to a post-labour society? This is a question politicians haven't been addressing.

Furthermore, robots are programmed by humans, and no human is perfect, so neither is our programming. Engineers have to consider how they program robotic entities when it comes to ethical and moral reasoning. Is it possible to program every potential moral quandary and the corresponding generally understood "correct" course of action, even with the help of machine learning? Computers do not currently have sufficient programming to pose the same kind of robust "what if" scenarios that humans can because they are constrained by the amount of information they have access to and how they are told to interact with that information. Humans, however, can make things up, and consider scenarios that would make no sense to a logic-based computer. As a result, humans can ask questions or make connections that computers currently can't. Computers are unlikely to ask, "What don't I know that I don't know?" Whereas humans are always seeking new information and considering possible outcomes. Is it possible to program computers to make these same considerations?

If we consider the *iRobot* movie adaptation, the main character has a hatred of robots because, after an accident, the robot who arrives on the scene decides to save him, an adult man, rather than save a 12-year-old girl because it calculated that his chances of survival were higher and prioritized his rescue. Like this character, many people disagree with the robot's reasoning and believe that young people should be prioritized in a situation like this because they have more life potential than a middle-aged person. Of course, there are others who disagree and side with the robot's logic. Given this disagreement, how should we program robots and AIs to act in situations where a moral or ethical decision needs to be made? We will explore this more in the section about self-driving cars.

We also have to consider how AI and robots can affect our behavior and future as humans. Stephen Hawking commented in an interview in 2014 that human evolution is so slow that AI would eventually surpass us in intelligence and capability. What then? Elon Musk calls AI "our biggest existential threat," and even Bill Gates is worried about the technology. There is an interesting theory called the *uncanny valley* which says that on the graph of how close something is to looking human, there is a spot called the uncanny valley where the image or creation looks real but there is just something *off* about it. Once it passes this point and becomes even more human-looking, the feeling goes away. The question is: should robots be designed to be approachable but distinctly robotic, or be as human as possible? Studies have shown time and time again that we need to interact with fellow humans to survive. If robots are integrated into society, we may see a decline in sociability and emotional intelligence because so much of our daily interaction is with robots. As more robots take over tasks previously done by humans, we also risk losing a lot of our technical skills and aptitudes. Evolutionary biologists posit that, at one point, humans had a much better innate sense of direction because we were a nomadic species. But once we discovered agriculture and could grow our own food rather than finding it, we eventually lost this ability because we didn't use it anymore. Could mass robotic automation cause a huge divide in intelligence and competence? How will we spend our time when most work is done by robots, and what skills will we gain or lose?

It's important to distinguish AI and machine learning from consciousness and sentience. While the former are completely mechanical processes based on advanced computer programming, consciousness and sentience implies some amount of self-awareness and individuality. So long as AIs don't become self-aware and develop sentience, many people believe they are just objects and don't have any inherent rights as such. Most would agree that this is ethically and morally acceptable. We don't feel sad throwing away an old phone the same way we do when we have to put down a pet. Our phones don't have feelings or self-awareness. This is the same for robots and AIs. Even if they can simulate emotions, these are simply cause and effect reactions based on lines of code in their programming. But, is this fair? An interesting exploration of this debate can be found on the TV show *Star Trek: The Next Generation* with the character Data, who is an android. In the episode "Measure of a Man," the story focuses around court proceedings trying to answer the question of whether Data has rights or not. Is he merely a sophisticated piece of machinery owned by the Federation, or is he an independent being deserving of respect and freedom from experimentation he does not consent to? The episode eventually concludes that Data has the right to choose what happens to him, thus giving him the same rights as humans. Would a real-world case on this issue go the same way? We won't know until it happens.

AUTONOMOUS VEHICLES

While the first thing you likely think of when you see *"autonomous vehicles"* is a self-driving car, any vehicle can technically be made autonomous. In fact, some transportation vehicles, like airplanes, are already primarily piloted by automated systems. Autonomous vehicles use a variety of sensor technology to assess their surroundings, plot courses, and perform safely. These are usually some combination of radar, GPS, proximity sensors, odometry, and inertial measurement units, among others. The sensors send their information to the internal computer, which in turn runs all of the mechanical parts that allow the vehicle to actually move. With commercially available self-driving cars just on the horizon, ethical and practical concerns have been commonly discussed in the public discourse so that we can prepare for this new wave of technology.

There is a difference between *autonomous* and *automated,* and confusion between the two has contributed to some of the controversy surrounding self-driving vehicles. Autonomous means that the entity is self-governing. An autonomous vehicle can adapt to changing surroundings and is a highly complex system that will be constantly reassessing the situation and reacting accordingly. Automation, on the other hand, is a much more linear and limited process. Something that is automated is simply controlled by a mechanical process, but it is limited in the kind of adaptations it can make to new situations. Consider the autopilot in your car. Despite the implications in the name, all this automated system does is maintain a set speed for you. You are still required to steer and be in control of the rest of the vehicle. The automation is merely there to make longer drives on freeways, where you need to keep a consistent speed, more comfortable. Automation and autonomy also differ greatly from existing driver assist functions like blind spot detection, self-correcting lane management, and auto-breaking when an obstacle is detected. These automated responses are directly related to specific sensory input and only activate under certain conditions. Autonomous vehicles are in control of these functions as well as everything else, all at the same time.

The benefits to self-driving vehicles connected to the IoT network are numerous. The biggest one is safety. Unlike humans, computers cannot fall asleep, don't experience fatigue, aren't distracted by loud music or phone calls, and can process sensory input from all directions at once and react in a split second, taking action when a human would still be processing the information. Experts and the consulting firm McKinsey & Company have estimated that full transition to self-driving vehicles could likely "eliminate 90% of all auto accidents in the United States." This would save billions of dollars in property damage, healthcare costs, and accident response, as well as thousands of lives, every year. The economy would do very well as a result. Despite some of the misinformation spreading online, the self-driving cars currently being road tested have experienced almost no collisions, and the ones they have been in were predominantly caused by human error.

With people free from having to pay attention to the road, they will always be passengers, leaving them to get some extra work done or simply relax. For those with disabilities or other impairments such as the elderly or chronically ill, autonomous vehicles would also provide an opportunity for more mobility. They would no longer have to rely solely on friends and family or public transit and taxi services. With the need for driver interface equipment eliminated, the interior of the vehicle could also be redesigned, allowing for greater safety in the unlikely event of a collision, as well as greater comfort and flexibility.

Another benefit predicted as a result of fully autonomous vehicles is reduced traffic. If all vehicles on the road could talk to each other and to the related systems such as traffic lights, cars could anticipate road conditions further in advance, allowing them to maintain higher speeds for longer. They could also more accurately predict potential gridlock situations, stopping to avoid blocking an intersection and compounding the congestion. There is even the chance to eliminate the need for traffic lights all together. While crossings would still need to be in place for pedestrians, cars that talk to each other could plan their crossing through an intersection without having to stop if they don't need to. Intersections would work more like 4-way stops but without the mandatory stop. Less stopping and slowing means traffic flows better. These traffic improvements will also result in improved fuel economy and reduced environmental impact. Some people dispute this, saying that increased convenience would encourage people to travel more, thus offsetting the reduced fuel consumption. However, with the rise of the autonomous car, we are seeing a similar rise in the popularity and efficiency of electric vehicles. If these two technologies converge, the environment will thank us for it.

One of the issues we face as self-driving cars hit the market is the transition from a fully hands-on fleet to a mixed autonomous and hands-on fleet before we get to a fully autonomous. There will be times during this transition where driving is likely to be slightly more dangerous. Different car manufacturers may try to employ their own proprietary self-driving system and try to manage a unique system to try and flush out the competition and keep profits growing. Unfortunately, without a uniform system of communication across the board, self-driving cars will behave differently and may have difficulty reacting to or anticipating the actions of other autonomous vehicles. Mix that in with hands-on vehicles still on the road, and accidents will likely still be a regular occurrence. Luckily, many manufacturers have considered this problem and have actually turned to open-source software that will allow everyone to have access to the same driving system. It will also allow more programming experts to enhance the software to make sure it stays safe and free of bugs and security holes.

There is the chance that short-term company interests will outweigh long-term safety interests, as we recently saw with Boeing. Two crashes happened within the course of six months, both involving the same kind of Boeing aircraft. Investigations into the crashes uncovered a horrifying detail: the cockpits lacked crucial safety overrides because Boeing charged extra for them and claimed they were optional. This was despite knowing that the software in the new model could sometimes experience a bug that caused the autopilot to incorrectly determine the plane was at risk of stalling and adjust the pitch to compensate. The safety feature they charged extra for was a button that pilots could press in the event this bug occurred erroneously to override the automatic correction. In the midst of widespread backlash, Boeing is now making this feature standard on their aircraft in an effort to try and rebuild their reputation. Self-driving cars are at risk for suffering similar mismanagement by negligent manufacturers. Hopefully, the use of the open-sourced software will allow for greater oversight and accountability.

But, despite this precaution, there is still the chance for interference from bad actors, as with any digital technology. Engineers and programmers will have to be especially vigilant about protecting driving networks from invasion and sabotage. Another technical challenge faced in the development of autonomous cars is the need for highly advanced AI and sensor systems. While the systems existing now have proven incredibly effective on freeways and in average driving conditions, they have had difficulty in chaotic environments like the downtown areas of big cities. These sensor systems also need to be catered to work in a variety of weather conditions. In places that get a lot of snow, trying to drive through a foot of fresh snow may cause certain systems to simply quit because they don't know how to process the incoming information. Map and navigation systems will also need to be constantly updated as cities change and grow so that the network can continue functioning properly.

Autonomous vehicles also face cultural and social pushback. Uncertainty will cause fear, and while this fear is justified, there is a risk for overregulation and unreasonable restrictions in response. This could delay manufacturers from getting self-driving cars on the road, which will prevent them from gathering valuable real-world testing information to help them improve the systems to alleviate the initial fears. As with robotics and AI, autonomous vehicles will also cause the loss of driving-related jobs like in taxi services and the trucking industry. Handling that transition will be a significant piece in the successful implementation of self-driving vehicles.

Researchers at MIT have anticipated another problem we looked at in our discussion of robotics, and that is the difficulty of programming morals into machines when people have such varying beliefs on what is right and wrong. They have created a survey called the "Moral Machine" that people can take in order to gather data on what the majority of people believe is the right thing to do in a number of moral dilemmas self-driving cars might face. The scenarios are procedurally generated and involve a self-driving car carrying randomly assigned passengers from humans of various genders and ages, and potentially pets like cats and dogs, that determines it cannot stop safely before the upcoming crosswalk. The crosswalk is populated by a set of random pedestrians and you have to decide if the car turns into the oncoming lane, hitting barriers and killing the passengers, or continues on and kills the pedestrians. At the end, you will be shown how your choices on who to save compare to the average responses already gathered. It is an interesting and tangible thought experiment in human and machine ethics and encourages deeper thinking about self-driving cars.

SOCIAL JUSTICE ISSUES

Social justice has become a loaded phrase in modern culture. Because we are primarily focused on technology and cyberspace, we won't be unpacking social justice in its wider context here. But we should still define it and consider how it fits into ethics, technology, and the Internet. Social justice is a concept that concerns itself primarily with the inherent nature of the human right to justice and equality. It asserts that relations between individuals and societies should be based on mutual respect and fair treatment. Social justice puts the responsibility for a just society on everyone, saying each group and individual has a part to play. However, varying perspectives on what justice and fairness look like to any given group or society make social justice a difficult issue in practice, even if it doesn't seem it in definition. Various competing social, religious, commercial, financial, and political agendas make establishing a core consensus of values nearly impossible, especially if no group is willing to compromise with another. Access to the Internet makes connecting with likeminded people incredibly easy and mobilizing them for or against a cause as quick as sending out a tweet.

The Internet, social media in particular, has given rise to extreme division over social justice and those who say its basic premises align most clearly with their beliefs about equality and fairness. In the late 20th century, the term *social justice warrior* was used to describe people who were activists for social progress and was primarily neutral or complementary. However, the term morphed with the rise of online activism and the connotation dramatically shifted sometime around 2011 when it was used on Twitter. It became a derogatory name, used typically by those who align more with generally conservative beliefs, to refer to the activists whose beliefs are in direct opposition with theirs. This has resulted in the shorthand, SJW, and is used to insult those who champion inclusivity, diversity, equality for minorities, and feminism, among others.

People who have studied the use of the term SJW as a pejorative have found evidence to suggest that it started as a more nuanced insult that was meant to refer to disingenuous *slacktivists*. Slacktivists are people who use the convenience of the Internet, online petitions, and Twitter shouting matches to pretend they are making a difference in order to feel good about themselves. This is also referred to as performative activism. It is also commonly associated with companies who use popular social justice causes as a way to create emotional connections in their advertising. Thus, SJW was a name meant to insult their selfish motivations and call attention to their hypocrisy. Unfortunately, ideological extremists have hijacked the term and now use it to dismiss social justice issues anytime someone brings them up. These extremists often feel like social progress is simply a veiled attempt to infringe on their free speech and the Internet has allowed this myth to spread and results in misinformation from confirmation bias (see Chapter V).

The Internet is, for better or for worse, the ultimate public forum. It is now the main stage for conversations of social issues to be played out. Virtue-signalling, humble-brag, snowflake, call-out culture, feminazi, race card, SJW—these are all parts of the digital discussion around social justice. What used to take place inside and in front of government buildings has moved into cyberspace and given rise to a whole host of philosophical and dialectical terms and definitions that will forever shape the way we discuss social justice and progress.

Chapter V: Professional Ethics

MORAL OBLIGATIONS, LEGAL LIABILITY, AND ACCOUNTABILITY OF CORPORATIONS

From corporate lobbyists trying to buy legislation which will make it easier for them to cut corners and turn a profit, to data leaks and privacy scandals, to class action lawsuits and social media prosecution, it can seem like capitalism, the law, and morality are at odds with each other these days. The interplay between these different systems is a cycle that doesn't show signs of stopping any time soon. However, we can still look at the ways in which corporations are responsible for their actions. It's important to understand the differences between moral obligations, legal liability, and accountability of corporations.

Moral responsibility is a form of blame, and companies or individuals, through admitting fault in the situation, are acknowledging that they are to blame for whatever the breach of moral obligation was. This *does not* necessarily mean that they will be held liable for the situation or that they will have to provide some measure of accountability or recompense. As a result, it is more often individuals that end up taking the blame in situations where moral or ethical codes have been violated. This is because corporations and governments are large entities, and oftentimes, the individual who broke the code did so of their own volition. In cases where they were actually instructed to act unethically, they usually face an uphill battle to prove it and it becomes the entity's word against theirs.

Liability is an entirely legal term sometimes referred to as "strict liability." This differs from responsibility and morality in that you can be held liable for something even though you may not have been directly responsible for the situation. For example, most states have laws that hold the property owner liable for any injury sustained on their property. This has been used, controversially, in cases of home invasion where a homeowner injured the invader in trying to defend their families and property. The homeowner is sometimes found guilty and required to pay the perpetrator for the injuries despite not having been directly responsible for the invader's decision to enter their home illegally. The morality of this is pretty clear, that the invader was in the wrong, but the liability is on the homeowner. It's important to note that in cases where a person or company is held liable for something, they are not necessarily being blamed or held at fault for the incident. The law is there to be applied to facts, regardless of the social circumstances.

Accountability refers to instances when an entity or individual is required to answer for a wrongdoing, though not necessarily through legal proceedings. This is often the case where a person or group has authority over a perpetrator and, for whatever reason, that person cannot answer for their own wrongdoing alone. For example, parents are often held responsible for their children's behavior and therefore bear the consequences for whatever happened. If a young student becomes aggressive toward a teacher or other student, it is the parents who ultimately have to do something about it; they apologize to the staff and other parents and have to find a way to prevent the situation from happening again. The child is liable for the aggression and is morally responsible, but the parents have to take the most steps to make it right because they are the ones with the maturity and capability to do so.

When it comes to corporations and digital issues, there are plenty of examples of times where the company was held morally responsible, legally liable, accountable, or some combination of all three. Perhaps the most famous one in recent memory has to do with the credit-reporting agency Equifax. In 2017, Equifax announced that upwards of 143 million people in the U.S. may have been affected by a cyberattack that resulted in hackers having access to social security numbers, past and current addresses, passport numbers, driver's license numbers, and some credit card information. While this hack was disturbing news in and of itself, even more distressing was that Equifax waited just over six weeks to announce the breach. That meant that for a month and a half, bad actors had access to people's data and identity theft could have already happened without users being able to take extra steps to protect themselves in light of the breach.

A few things happened after the breach was announced. Equifax first set up a registry where people could put in their information to have the system check if they were one of the theft victims. They then also offered free protection packages for a year to those who signed up. This step was controversial, however, because if you forgot to cancel after that year, you would be automatically charged for and enrolled in another year. People were upset about this because the ethical optics of charging potential victims for a service they shouldn't have even needed if Equifax had been more diligent in protecting their data in the first place was not good for the company. Especially because experts predicted that due to the amount of data stolen, it could potentially take decades before all of the victims were secure again. Furthermore, Equifax made it mandatory that if you opted in to the protection trial, you waived your right to sue the company for damages as a result of the breach unless you sent them a written letter within 30 days of signing up. Understandably, many people were not a fan of this ultimatum.

Unfortunately, more than a year after the hack, very little has been done and Equifax has faced almost no consequences. A law was proposed to impose a fine on credit-reporting agencies who experience a breach of security, but it didn't pass. Equifax claimed that, since the breach, it has spent over $200 million on cybersecurity improvements, including closing the vulnerability that led to the breach. In January of 2019, more than a year after the hack was announced, a U.S. judge allowed for a number of class-action lawsuits against Equifax to proceed, but Equifax has intentions of continuing to fight to have them dismissed. Equifax has thus far accepted some of the blame (moral responsibility) and has taken some action to be accountable (extra security measures, free protection packages), but they have yet to face any strict liability, so we will have to wait and see what happens from here.

MORAL RESPONSIBILITIES OF IT PROFESSIONALS

When most people think of an IT professional, they think of technical support. While tech support is a part of IT, it goes beyond that to include software and hardware engineers, network administrators, computer repair technicians, as well as professors and instructors in these fields. For a lot of us, computers are basically magic boxes and networks are intangible and invisible roads. IT professionals create these systems and help the rest of us laypeople keep them working. That level of expertise is what makes them professionals. It is also what makes codes of ethics and conduct so important. The guidelines for appropriate actions help enforce accountability in these professions because the rest of us may not know what is right and wrong intuitively. When we have access to a code of ethics, however, we can more easily assert ourselves and know when something is unethical. This applies to every profession, not just computers and IT.

What makes IT professionals unique is that they are often dealing with "safety-critical systems." A safety-critical system is one that provides the opportunity to do significant harm or good, whether through direct actions on the part of the professional, allowance by the professional, or influence from the professional. These systems are any that can directly impact people's lives and safety, such as air traffic control systems or mass transportation systems. IT professionals aren't always working with safety-critical systems, but they are always handling equipment and information that is important to daily life and operations for companies and individuals. This may also include confidential or personal data.

Don Gotterbarn, a computer ethics researcher, asserts that the focus of any guidelines intended for IT professionals should be professional responsibility and accountability.

Initially, he claimed that computer ethics should be isolated from broader moral and social ethical concerns. Critics, however, have pointed out that the ubiquity of computers and the Internet necessitate a more comprehensive view. Despite this criticism, Gotterbarn's model seems to be the most robust for creating effective codes for computer and IT professionals to follow. He says that codes serve three main purposes. They act as codes of ethics, codes of conduct, and codes of practice. Ethics refers to the moral ideals the profession strives to uphold. Conduct refers to an individual's behavior and mental approach to the job. Practice refers to the actual work and operations in a given field and describes the imperatives unique to the profession.

The Institute for Electrical and Electronics Engineers Computer Society (IEEE-CS) and the Association for Computing Machinery (ACM) are two of the largest governing bodies for IT professionals. Before the 1990s, these two organizations had their own professional codes for members which were specific to individual careers within the computer profession. However, IEEE and ACM decided it was time for a more comprehensive code that could be applied to all computer and IT professionals to help standardize expectations of ethics conduct, and practice. This joint code is called the Software Engineering Code of Ethics and Professional Practice (SECEPP). You can find the entire code online, but it starts with a core preamble of eight main imperatives on eight key aspects of the profession. These are quoted directly from the SECEPP itself.

1. *Public:* Software engineers shall act consistently with the public interest.
2. *Client and Employers:* Software engineers shall act in a manner that is in the best interests of their client and employer, consistent with the public interest.
3. *Product:* Software engineers shall ensure that their products and related modifications meet the highest professional standards possible.
4. *Judgment:* Software engineers shall maintain integrity and independence in their professional judgment.
5. *Management:* Software engineering managers and leaders shall subscribe to and promote an ethical approach to the management of software development and maintenance.
6. *Profession:* Software engineers shall advance the integrity and reputation of the profession consistent with the public interest.
7. *Colleagues:* Software engineers shall be fair to and supportive of their colleagues.
8. *Self:* Software engineers shall participate in lifelong learning regarding the practice of their profession and shall promote an ethical approach to the practice of the profession.

Each of these eight principles are broken down into more specific guidelines such as "accepting full responsibility for their own work" and "be fair and avoid deception in all statements, particularly public ones." The SECEPP emphasizes computer professionals' duty to the public, which is important because, as we mentioned, computers are largely mysterious to most users. We can't verify any work they do for us because, if we could, it would mean we could have done the work ourselves. Therefore, any professional code in the discipline must be especially aware of public perception and public interest and demand integrity from its members.

IT and computer professionals have access to safety-critical systems, confidential information, and other data that could greatly affect people's lives. Much like those in the fields of medicine and education, they are therefore held to a high standard of ethics, conduct, and practice to ensure that this information and these systems are handled properly and thoughtfully.

But is there ever a time when it is more ethical to break the rules set out for you by an employer? When a situation like this arises, the person is often referred to as a whistle-blower. Whistle-blowing isn't inherently unethical nor are the people blowing the whistles disloyal. In fact, when done through careful consideration and in situations where staying silent would do serious harm, whistle-blowing is often the most correct course of action for a person to take. Experts theorize that the 1986 Space Shuttle *Challenger* disaster would have likely been avoided if the engineers took their concerns about launching on a cool day to the press when their superiors ignored their warnings. Public pressure could have delayed the launch and saved the lives of the *Challenger* crew members.

It is important in discussions of whistle-blowing to also consider the difference between being morally *permitted* to blow the whistle and morally *required* to do so. It is generally believed that one is permitted to blow the whistle when they are sure that a situation will cause serious harm to the public, have already reported it to their supervisor, and pursued all of the available avenues within their company and still received no support for their concern. At this point, they are morally permitted to go outside of the company to bring attention to the issue and hopefully force an investigation into their concern. However, to be morally obligated to blow the whistle, the person should also be able to prove their concern with available and reliable documented evidence as well as be sure that going public will bring about the change required to fix the concern. Most whistle-blowers are protected by the Occupational Safety and Health Administration (OSHA), who can investigate incidents of whistle-blowing to see if the employee was justified or not. If they are, their employer is prohibited from taking action against them. They may also seek protection under the First Amendment, depending on the nature of the incident and their employee code of conduct. Government whistle-blowers are protected by the Whistleblower Protection Act of 1989.

Perhaps the most famous whistle-blower in U.S. history is Edward Snowden. In 2013, a former CIA employee was hired by the NSA by a contractor. In May of that year, he flew to Hong Kong and, in June, he shared thousands of classified documents to three journalists: Glenn Greenwald, Laura Poitras, and Ewen MacAskill. The documents he released largely pertained to the security legislation we discussed at length in Chapter I (*Government Surveillance*) and Chapter II (*Collection and Use of Personal Data: National Security*), those being the surveillance sections of FISA and the Patriot Act. Snowden's actions shook the nation to its core and triggered a debate over mass surveillance that persists today (see Chapter II, *National Security*). Because Snowden's disclosure of information related to surveillance that impacts national security, federal prosecutors charged him with theft of government property and two counts of violating the Espionage Act of 1917. Due to the provisions of the Espionage Act, Snowden would not be allowed to defend himself in a trial with a jury, so he would likely be convicted. Snowden is currently living in Russia with an asylum visa set to expire in 2020 unless extended. Public opinions on Snowden's actions remain divided and he is largely condemned by government officials.

THE ROLE OF THE PRESS

We live in a time of transition for news media. Thanks to the accessibility of the Internet and the availability of word processing and video capture tools, anyone can purport to report the news and contribute, positively or negatively, to the news cycle. What they may not realize is that true journalists are trained to research and present the news and are subject to a professional code of their own, referred to as journalistic integrity. Journalism has also been complicated by news aggregators and the need to drive traffic to websites to make ad revenue and please investors.

First, let's briefly look at the basic journalism ethics and standards taught in journalism courses and, ideally, enforced by employers. Perhaps the foremost body of journalists in the U.S. is the Society of Professional Journalists (SPJ) and they have created four main guiding principles:

1. Seek truth and report it: Ethical journalism should be accurate and fair. Ethical journalists should be honest and courageous in gathering, reporting and interpreting information.
2. Minimize harm: Ethical journalism treats sources, subjects, colleagues and members of the public as human beings deserving of respect.
3. Act independently: The highest and primary obligation of ethical journalism is to serve the public.
4. Be accountable: Ethical journalism means taking responsibility for one's work and explaining one's decisions to the public.

Unfortunately, no journalistic principle exists to discourage the overreporting of bad news. In our discussion of individual behavior on the Internet and people's use of social media, we looked at how outrage culture has come to be a big part of online discourse.

Some experts think that this is related to the disproportioned reporting of bad news that started with television and newspaper media outlets. It's no secret that views and clicks go up drastically when there is bad news to report. After the attacks on September 11, 2001, people consumed an average of eight hours of coverage each over the following few days. That is an average shift at work dedicated entirely to upsetting news. It can be easy to get caught up in the rush of bad news and drama because it triggers our fear response. Brains are easily tricked into thinking something is real and immediate, even if it isn't. It's why we can cry at a movie or book even though we know it's fake. When we see bad news, we immediately start worrying that it could happen to us or someone we love, and we want to do something about it. Whereas with good news, we feel good after we hear it, and then we move on with our day. Maybe we will be a little nicer to the barista at the coffee shop or hold the door for people even though we have to be somewhere, but our brains have a hard time holding onto good news and feelings. In short, bad news triggers more engagement than good news.

Furthermore, the news is supposed to be about things that happen, and good things aren't often active events, but rather passive states of being. For example, it's not news that there wasn't a terrorist attack yesterday because nothing happened. Peace was just peace as the neutral state of being. It's only when that peace is broken that something has occurred and thus is reported on. This isn't always the case though. Think about all of those hero stories where a child falls into a river and someone jumps in to save them, or a teenager starts a not-for-profit making blankets for children going through chemotherapy. These are good things that happen, but the story also doesn't develop beyond that. "Teenager Still Making Blankets" isn't a catchy headline, whereas "Ten More Found Dead in Earthquake Rubble" unfortunately is.

News anchors and journalists can also accidentally contribute negatively to a situation despite their good intentions by over-reporting on inaccurate claims and "fake news." Studies show that the more someone hears something repeated, the more likely they are to believe it, even if it is immediately discredited. So, the more we consume news reports by journalists just trying their best to give the facts of the situation and present both sides of the story, the more we can actually become confused and not actually know what is true and what is false. In looking at how different sources cover news about President Trump, Sophia McClennen, the associate director for the School of International Affairs at Penn State, says, "The news media…seems like it has to take [ridiculous claims] seriously in order to be taken seriously." In other words, news anchors and traditional journalists will approach a clearly outrageous and false claim, such as that Trump had the largest inauguration gathering of all time, with the same seriousness and credibility as a story about a plane crash. In an effort to be unbiased and appear non-partisan in the facts, news media outlets will correctly report the inaccuracy of the claim and then the truth of the situation. Except, rather than move on, they will talk to experts, and spokespeople, and representatives, hosting debates about the truthfulness of the claim, and repeating it over and over again during a single news cycle.

What this fixation does is create doubt in the viewer's mind that the claim is indeed false. The news media is scared to just say the claim is wrong and move on because they are worried about receiving criticism for "not doing their due diligence" by investigating further, as well as not having click-/view-worthy content for the rest of the hour. But, by not rejecting the claim as a flat-out lie not based in reality and moving on, the press actually ends up feeding into the lie. Giving it more airtime only lends credence to it by saying that it needs to be talked about when it really doesn't. Viewers then end up thinking about the claim so much they ask the same questions as the debaters: "Maybe there really is something to this claim?" By giving a voice to the objectively wrong side of the debate, journalists and anchors end up creating a "passive news report" that doesn't actually push the needle one way or the other and confuses viewers into being less sure of the truth.

The news media faces an internal ethical dilemma here: do they continue to "do their due diligence" in cases where a claim is clearly baseless from the outset, or do they risk criticism in order to be more responsible for the subconscious effects of their reporting? Which is the more responsible and ethical thing to do? If we look at the principles for ethical journalism from above, one could argue that Principle 2, minimize harm, demands they go with the latter option. But one could also argue that in order to satisfy Principle 1, seek truth and report it, they are obligated to continue to give fake news a voice in their reporting. At this moment, there seems to be no easy answer to this question.

Thanks to the Internet, the news is more accessible than ever. You can read newspapers and magazines from all over the world and be plugged into the global news cycle. But, given the prevalence of bad news, this becomes one of the many double-edged swords of the Internet that we've looked at. The Internet makes the 24-hour news cycle even more prolific than before. Anyone can talk about developing stories and unfortunately, this means journalists may not be able to adequately follow the first principle, "seek truth and report it." In rushing to get to a story before too many other outlets get it, journalists may cut corners by not doing their due diligence in following a lead, interviewing all of the parties involved, or seeking more points of view (e.g. witnesses and video evidence).

This happened with the "MAGA Hat Kid" in early 2019. People were quick to jump to conclusions to report on the video that appeared to show a teenager in a MAGA hat smirking condescendingly at a Native American man drumming at a rally while his classmates imitated him and shouted. People demonized him, calling him a racist and blaming Trump's politics for the situation. The next day, however, new video and reports came out, showing that a radical Israelite group actually started the whole thing by calling the teenagers names and harassing them. The teens responded, some by doing their school cheer, some by shouting vulgar things in return. The drummer tried to come between the two groups while playing a song about peace and the boy ended up in front of him in the crowd. Whether you believe the boy is a racist for his facial expression or just a teenager confused by what was happening and reacting awkwardly, the questions remains: would you still believe that if the information had come out in a different way?

The press has a duty to present the truth and do as little harm as possible, but the Internet has complicated that mission and sometimes journalists make mistakes that severely harm reputations and change lives. It remains to be seen if guidelines and laws for journalists will change as we tackle this challenge.

SOCIAL MEDIA – POSITIVE REINFORCEMENT AND DISSEMINATION OF UNFOUNDED INFORMATION

We've already looked at how the Internet is an empowering tool that allows individuals of all backgrounds, beliefs, and educations to create and share content online. We also discussed how this can have both a positive and negative effect on public discourse and culture. In this section we will dig deeper into the problems with online echo chambers, confirmation bias, dissemination of unfounded information, and how companies and lawmakers are trying to tackle them.

Let's start by defining these problems. *Confirmation bias* is a concept in psychology that refers to the human tendency to seek out and prefer information that confirms, or supports, pre-existing beliefs and ideas. Confirmation bias is one of the biggest problems facing online culture and social media today. The Internet puts so much information at our fingertips, and yet we still have difficulty accepting or acknowledging facts that dispute our already held notions. Instead, we seek out echo chambers, or groups of likeminded individuals who will reaffirm our beliefs and tell us that we are right, and the rest of the world is wrong. This cognitive bias can be incredibly harmful, as we will see in a moment when we look at the issue of Facebook and vaccine misinformation.

The dissemination of unfounded information is quite simply the creation and spreading of falsehoods. These falsehoods could be deliberately crafted lies intended to serve a bias or they could be mistakes resulting from faulty reasoning influenced by biased thinking. For example, most of us have probably heard that we only use 10 percent of our brains. Scientists have proven this to be categorically false and brain scans show us that the vast majority of a person's brain is active at all times. Most people no longer believe this harmless myth and it mostly just finds its way into fictional movies and books.

Some falsehoods, however, aren't quite so harmless. In 1997, Andrew Wakefield published an article in a medical journal claiming the MMR (measles-mumps-rubella) vaccine caused autism in children. The paper almost single-handedly ignited widespread vaccine hesitation in parents and has been held up as the main proof that children should not be given the MMR vaccine. Questions about Wakefield's methodology and ethics became more common as the study spread, and in 2010, following an investigation, the medical journal retracted the paper and Wakefield had his medical license revoked for acting "dishonestly and irresponsibly" in publishing the study. His methods were found to be unscientific, his procedure unethical, and his results have only been replicated by similarly flawed studies. Since then, innumerable studies have shown there is no link between autism and the MMR vaccine and that autism is not something a person gets, but rather something they *have* from birth.

The damage had already been done though, and thousands of parents are opting out of vaccines despite the mountain of evidence supporting the MMR vaccine and the success of herd immunity. In the previous section, we looked at the role of the press and how repeated exposure to false information will make you more likely to think it might be true, even though you already know it isn't. What happens on social media is that this incorrect information gets spread by everyone at such a rapid rate and with such voracity that the same effect occurs. This is one of the biggest dangers facing social media users and is caused by thoughtless and biased sharing, and this is having real-world consequences.

Currently, a growing number of cities in the United States are facing major measles outbreaks and experts are attributing them almost entirely to vaccine hesitancy and vaccine misinformation. Facebook groups and posts are the largest method by which vaccine misinformation is spread, so health experts, lawmakers, and concerned parents alike called on Facebook to take action to limit the spread of false information. They have since announced that they will be reducing the visibility of these posts as well as rejecting any ads or sponsored posts that contain said content. They will also push the content down in searches so accurate information will appear first. Since Facebook owns Instagram, the policies will also be enforced there. Similarly, YouTube is taking action by preventing anti-vaccine content from appearing in any trending or recommended pages, pushing the content lower in searches, not allowing such content to be monetized, and every video featuring vaccine misinformation will have a link to a reputable source, such as the World Health Organization, underneath it. Some activists and experts are calling for Facebook and YouTube to do more by banning anti-vaccine groups and content all together, but others argue that such a route could violate free speech laws if done without careful planning and implementation (see Chapter III).

The solution to the dissemination of misinformation, according to experts, is not silencing those who make false claims, but encouraging individuals to question everything they read and hear and to do their own investigations into a subject before coming to a conclusion. There are several sites and services dedicated to fact-checking claims that are helpful starting points, such as Snopes.com, FactCheck.org, and PolitiFact. It's also important to be aware of how to identify bias in a source and read beyond the headline of an article. An easy acronym to remember is CRAAP; **C**urrency (is the source recent enough to be considered valid), **R**elevance (is the information presented germane to the discussion), **A**uthority (does the source demonstrate proper due diligence in its assertions), **A**ccuracy (is the source free from false or inaccurate information that may indicate a bias or lack of integrity), **P**urpose (for what reason was this source created: to inform or to persuade or to serve a specific agenda). Tackling the dissemination of unfounded information takes effort both on the part of the social media platform and the users themselves.

NET NEUTRALITY

One of the most contentious debates we face in the digital era is over net neutrality. If there is one thing to take away from our discussions so far, it is that the Internet is like our oceans: vast and accessible worldwide, full of amazing wonders and opportunities, but also largely unknown and unmonitored, with plenty of dangers lurking below the surface. Net neutrality is one of those talking points that we can discuss for hours and not come to a consensus on. However, it is still worth discussing, as this term, and the concepts that it represents, is extremely important for the future of the Internet.

Ajit Pai is an American lawyer and current Chairman of the Federal Communications Commission (FCC). Against the wishes of the majority of the public, many experts, and several activist groups, Pai repealed net neutrality on June 11, 2018. The fights to uphold this repeal and to overturn it are ongoing, with both sides taking advantage of every actionable option. Despite the amount of press coverage, it's possible that many people are still not quite sure what net neutrality is and what the repeal means for individuals and businesses. In this section we are going to define net neutrality and look at the main points groups for and against it are using in their fights.

At the center of the debate over net neutrality is control over Internet usage, speed, and censorship. When net neutrality laws were in place, ISPs and other groups couldn't engage in practices that would result in extra paywalls, throttling (the act of slowing down a connection's speed deliberately), or the manipulation of access to information not profitable to the ISP. Net neutrality protects small businesses, freelancers, and start-ups by giving them a level playing field online. It places limits on sponsored content so that anyone with good search engine optimization and advertising can succeed online and experience the same traffic as larger companies without fear of throttling or suppression. Finally, it classifies the Internet as a utility like water and power, thus preventing ISPs from choosing who gets it or what speed based on how much they can pay.

One of the downsides to net neutrality is the amount of content that can be accessed without additional compensation to the creator, copyright holder, or ISP. Take Netflix as an example. For two monthly fees, you can use your unlimited Internet to stream hours of Netflix a day as well as check your email, post on Facebook, and leave a review for the restaurant you went to the other day. Looking at the usage versus the cost, ISPs are technically getting the short end of the stick as they are only being paid by you, and not by Netflix, meaning Netflix is essentially using their infrastructure for free. There was a time when every ISP had Internet packages that limited Internet use to a certain gigabyte cap, but net neutrality and demands from consumers for fairer prices, given the ubiquity of the Internet, changed that. Under net neutrality, ISPs are also required to charge high-use companies and individuals (such as Netflix, Google, Shopify, etc.) on the same grid as small households. This means places using significantly higher bandwidth every month are not paying "significantly" more than any other consumer. If this changed, ISPs would have more income to maintain and improve their infrastructure.

Those who support the repeal of net neutrality say that their primary concern is fair compensation for services rendered. ISPs provide an important service to people, yet see comparatively little in return. They also argue that net neutrality allows questionable content to flourish online. If ISPs had more control over what sites and content was allowed to pass through their servers, they could, in theory, filter out inappropriate and offensive content before people could access it. It's important to remember that illegal content is still illegal whether or not net neutrality in enforced, so this ISP censorship applies to content the ISP itself determines is inappropriate. Lastly, many of those who are against net neutrality, like Pai, claim that it is just political theater and repealing it will actually result in few changes due to other trade and communications laws, as well as business ethics.

What Pai proposed to replace the previous net neutrality rules was the Restoring Internet Freedom Order. It eliminated the rules against ISP throttling or blocking access to certain content and the rule against ISPs prioritizing their own content (or that of companies willing to pay them for better access). However, ISPs are required to disclose situations where they may be engaging in throttling or blocking. Oversight has thus shifted from the FCC to the Federal Trade Commission (FTC) and such practices will be judged on a case-by-case basis to determine if the action is anti-competitive.

As of this writing, the repeal of net neutrality is still very new, and we have yet to see any significant changes to ISPs or the Internet in either direction. Consumer advocacy groups are concerned that this lack of change is largely due to the wide public condemnation of the repeal and could change as the outrage fades and people move on from fighting for or arguing about net neutrality. Others, however, say that it is because ISPs have no plans to harm their consumers and are merely working on policies that will create a better Internet for all by encouraging fair compensation and access. We will have to wait and see what effect this has on the future of the Internet in the United States and if the ripples will be felt across the world as we explore this digital frontier.

Sample Test Questions

CHAPTER I

1) What are some of the kinds of crimes committed online?

   A) Theft
   B) Fraud
   C) Hardware sabotage
   D) All of the above

The correct answer is D:) All of the above. This is correct because all three kinds of crime listed can be committed via online avenues by hackers and virus programmers.

2) Which of the following options is NOT a cybersecurity method?

   A) Passwords
   B) Privacy screens for monitors
   C) Authentication
   D) None of the above

The correct answer is D:) None of the above. This is correct because passwords and authentication are listed in Chapter I of the text, and privacy screens help prevent your information from being stolen by people looking over your shoulder. Therefore, all three are methods of cybersecurity.

3) How does a firewall protect your device?

   A) By burning up viruses and bots before they reach your data
   B) By acting as a checkpoint for incoming signals and comparing them to a list of trusted or untrusted sources and acting accordingly
   C) By setting your device on fire when it detects a threat
   D) None of the above

The correct answer is B:) By acting as a checkpoint for incoming signals and comparing them to a list of trusted or untrusted sources and acting accordingly. As discussed in Chapter I, a firewall is a kind of digital gatekeeper for your device, protecting it from harmful malware.

4) Which of these statements correctly defines "privacy"?

    A) Being able to hide evidence of wrongdoing
    B) Personal right to have information and identity free from public attention
    C) Freedom to act with anonymity online
    D) None of the above

The correct answer is B:) Personal right to have information and identity free from public attention. Privacy, broadly speaking, is a person's right to keep their personal information, affiliations, beliefs, and actions, free from public attention. However, this right is limited, due to some instances requiring the loss of privacy, such as if an individual committed a crime.

5) Nissenbaum's privacy framework, contextual integrity, proposes that decisions be made using which two factors?

    A) Norms of formality, norms of policy
    B) Norms of etiquette, norms of distribution
    C) Norms of appropriateness, norms of distribution
    D) Norms of context, norms of appropriateness

The correct answer is C:) Norms of appropriateness, norms of distribution. Establishing the norms of appropriateness and distribution help people make decisions of what information is OK to share with whom and in what context.

6) Which sentence most accurately describes a privacy policy?

    A) A policy allowing you complete anonymity while utilizing an online system
    B) A policy that outlines the expectations for the user and provider of an online system regarding any information collected through that system
    C) A policy preventing a company from sharing information you have provided to its system to third parties
    D) A policy detailing how a user is expected to act while using an online system

The correct answer is B:) A policy that outlines the expectations for the user and provider of an online system regarding any information collected through that system. A privacy policy, also known as an End User Licensing Agreement (EULA) is a document that must be agreed to before utilizing an online system which lays out the expectations for the user (you) and the company with regard to how the company will collect, store, and utilize any information provided by the user.

7) What term is used to define the proper way to act online?

   A) Netiquette
   B) Forum Decorum
   C) The Net Code
   D) Civilspace

The correct answer is A:) Netiquette. A portmanteau of net and etiquette, netiquette is the widely accepted term used to describe the proper and polite manner of acting online.

8) Is digital piracy the same as theft?

   A) Yes, both involve the acquisition of something without compensation
   B) No, cyberspace has different rules because things aren't real
   C) No, but only if it's something small like one song or TV show episode
   D) Yes, but only if you download it; streaming doesn't count

The correct answer is A:) Yes, both involve the acquisition of something without compensation. No matter what justification you use, if you download or stream something that you should be paying for, it is considered stealing. This applies even in ethical gray areas where you would pay for something if you could.

9) Is blocking online ads theft because it means you are using a service without contributing to the site's ad revenue?

   A) Yes, if you want to use a website you should have to deal with ads if they have them so they can get proper compensation
   B) No, there is nothing wrong with blocking ads because one ad doesn't make enough of a difference to count as theft
   C) No, the law doesn't say anything about blocking ads, but the ethical question remains on whether it's wrong or not
   D) None of the above

The correct answer is C:) No, the law doesn't say anything about blocking ads, but the ethical question remains on whether it's wrong or not. While there aren't any laws saying that blocking ads is theft because of the reduced revenue, there is still a personal moral dilemma over not allowing ads and using websites for free.

10) What is an influencer with regard to social media?

    A) Someone who controls online policies regarding social media
    B) A group of individuals who propose and suggest new online trends or fads
    C) Individuals with large online followings who use their presence to effect greater changes in society
    D) Individuals with large online presences who are sponsored by companies to support or endorse the brand or product

The correct answer is D:) Individuals with large online presences who are sponsored by companies to support or endorse the brand or product. Online influencers are individuals who, either with the knowledge of their audience or not, are sponsored to create content to support or endorse a product or company.

11) What is "Native Advertising"?

    A) Advertising that modifies itself to include information about the location that the ad is being shown
    B) Advertising that originates from the location where it is being shown
    C) Advertising that is presented as content that would typically be expected from a platform or creator
    D) Advertising that focuses on the local individuals of a particular location

The correct answer is C:) Advertising that is presented as content that would typically be expected from a platform or creator. When advertising takes on the form of the typically expected content on a platform or from a creator, that is defined as native advertising.

12) Eileen loves posting on Instagram and recently shared a series of selfies showcasing a funky new lipstick shade. Normally, she gets over 100 likes on a post on the first day, but this one only got 79. This causes her to be incredibly embarrassed and she throws away the lipstick. What psychological theory best describes why she was so upset at getting fewer likes than normal?

    A) Narcissistic personality theory
    B) Ownership theory
    C) Social media effect theory
    D) Self-destructive behaviour theory

The correct answer is B:) Ownership theory. We don't know enough about Eileen to suspect she is a narcissist, but we can tell that the number of likes she gets is important to her. This behaviour can be explained by psychological ownership theory, which suggests humans have an innate urge to collect things.

13) Which of these statements accurately describes outrage culture?

   A) A reactionary mentality where individuals respond immediately to a perceived wrongdoing with anger and mob mentality
   B) A feeling that social media gives you the right to hold people and companies accountable for their actions
   C) People looking for things to be angry about so that they can feel good about taking action
   D) All of the above

The correct answer is D:) All of the above. All of these statements address different facets of online outrage culture.

14) Phillis works for a PR firm controlling a relatively large brand's Twitter account. One day, she accidentally tweets a photo intended for her own private Twitter on the company's Twitter feed. She almost immediately recognizes her mistake and deletes the tweet. In what ways could the tweet remain available even after it has been deleted and removed from the account?

   A) Website caches
   B) Screenshots
   C) Downloaded copies
   D) All of the above

The correct answer is D:) All of the above. Unlike in physical space, the digital nature of the Internet means that it is very easy to create copies, either intentionally (through screenshots or direct downloads) or not (through the caching systems of most web browsers), meaning that almost anything uploaded to the Internet is never truly deleted.

15) What is data mining?

   A) The recovery of lost data from damaged hardware
   B) The discovery of data or information from obscure or forgotten online systems
   C) The act of gathering mass quantities of data from individuals through online systems
   D) The act of breaking into someone's social media sites to discover secrets about their lives

The correct answer is C:) The act of gathering mass quantities of data from individuals through online systems. As described in the text, data mining involves the widescale gathering of information from online systems, such as websites, search engines, and social media platforms, as well as other digital signatures such as GPS.

16) What are the common uses of data mining?

    A) To assess and collect data about potential national threats
    B) To help drive and fine tune marketing and brand decisions
    C) To create packets of data to sell to aggregators for a profit
    D) Both A and B

The correct answer is D:) Both A and B. Data mining has many possible uses, both for active defence and for capitalistic enterprise.

17) Under the Protect America Act, when are governmental forces permitted to wiretap and collect data without a warrant?

    A) When the individual or individuals in question communicate with other native individuals about a potential target
    B) Whenever there is a potential threat to the U.S.
    C) When suspected individuals contact foreign terrorist suspects or groups
    D) When the threat is considered too high or immediate to allow for a warrant to be processed

The correct answer is C:) When suspected individuals contact foreign terrorist suspects or groups. Although large amounts of data are collected and recorded as per FISA, a warrant is needed in all cases except when a suspect makes contact with foreign terrorist suspects or groups.

18) Sally created a profile on the hot new dating website HyperDates. While creating her account, she provided her favorite bands, her name, and her email address, among other information. What type of data would this be considered?

    A) Explicit data
    B) Self-disclosed data
    C) Implicit data
    D) Expected data

The correct answer is A:) Explicit data. This data has been willingly and actively provided by Sally, and so is considered explicit data.

19) Tom is interested in cars and spends a good deal of each day watching reviews and test rides on YouTube. Lately, he's noticed that he has been receiving advertisements for various car companies and retailers before videos and in the sidebar. What type of data may have been used to suggest these types of ads?

A) Explicit data
B) Implicit data
C) Inferential data
D) Intrusive data

The correct answer is B:) Implicit data. This data was collected passively based on Tom's actions with an online system, and so is considered implicit data.

20) Which of the below options is not a way companies collect implicit data on consumers?

A) Web cookies
B) Third party data brokers
C) Surveys
D) Passive collection

The correct answer is C:) Surveys. Although all methods are used by companies to collect data on consumers, surveys are an example of explicit data collection, rather than implicit data collection.

21) How does data mining help protect you from fraud?

A) By monitoring your credit activity and location data, the system can detect purchases that are abnormal, put a hold on the transaction, and send you an alert
B) By asking for a PIN number when purchases are made
C) By using complex algorithms to calculate your fraud risk and acting on the results
D) By giving your data to private investigators who track your movements to verify purchases are made by you

The correct answer is A:) By monitoring your credit activity and location data, the system can detect purchases that are abnormal, put a hold on the transaction, and send you an alert. If you make a purchase by your home in New York City and two hours later the card is used in Brighton, U.K., the system will flag the purchase because a purchase is being made in another country.

CHAPTER II

1) Which option best describes what the CISA allows for?

    A) The sharing of all personal information between ISPs and government security agencies
    B) Providing governmental agencies with the freedom to access locked or protected hardware
    C) The sharing of information relating to cybersecurity threats between ISPs and government security agencies
    D) Providing government agencies with a direct connection to Internet traffic and information

The correct answer is C:) The sharing of information relating to cybersecurity threats between ISPs and government security agencies. CISA, or the Cybersecurity Information Sharing Act, allows for the creation of a system to communicate between ISPs and government agencies on issues regarding cybersecurity.

2) Due to their proximity, the U.S. and Canada have an established cybersecurity treaty between the two nations (the TFCA). What does this treaty permit?

    A) The free exchange of personal information regarding suspects of potential or enacted cyberattacks
    B) The sharing of collected communication and Internet histories between designated governmental agencies
    C) Accountability by the nation for the damages caused by an individual(s) who perpetuated the cybercrime
    D) There is no such treaty, as no nation currently has a major cybersecurity treaty with another country

The correct answer is D:) There is no such treaty, as no nation currently has a major cybersecurity treaty with another country. Although there are informal agreements and communication between countries, no major international treaties regarding the exchange of cybersecurity information currently exist.

3) Which countries compose the current "Five Eyes" group of digital intelligence sharing?

   A) U.S., Australia, New Zealand, U.K., Canada
   B) U.S., Russia, China, U.K., Canada
   C) U.S., U.K., France, China, Japan
   D) U.S., Japan, China, Canada, Russia

The correct answer is A:) U.S., Australia, New Zealand, U.K., Canada. As discussed in Chapter II, these five nations have formed an informal collection who frequently share information regarding cybercrime and security.

4) Which of the following is **NOT** a forbidden purpose of Canada's CSE (Communications Security Establishment)?

   A) To acquire and use information from the global information infrastructure for the purpose of providing foreign intelligence
   B) To provide advice, guidance, and services to help ensure the protection of electronic information and information infrastructures of importance to the Government of Canada
   C) To collect and record all incoming and outgoing communications across Canadian borders for the purposes of identification of potential cyberthreats
   D) To provide technical and operation assistance to federal law enforcement and security agencies in the performance of their lawful duties

The correct answer is C:) To collect and record all incoming and outgoing communications across Canadian borders for the purposes of identification of potential cyberthreats. Canada's cybercrime and security branch has many proscribed actions but keeping track of all communications traffic across the border is not among them.

5) What does the General Data Protection Regulation (GDPR) bill **NOT** require from companies operating within the EU?

   A) That all online data collection must be consented to by the user
   B) That users may revoke their agreement to terms regarding data collection at any time
   C) That they inform users and authorities of data breaches without undue delay
   D) That they divulge all third-party software/agencies used in the collection of data and use of that collected data

The correct answer is D:) That they divulge all third-party software/agencies used in the collection of data and use of that collected data. Although the GDPR does limit what companies are able to do with the collected data, they are not required to discuss all of the agencies and software utilized in the process of collection.

6) What are the most collected kinds of personal data?

    A) Phone records, including who contacted who, how long the call was, and when it occurred
    B) Internet history, including search history and what sites were visited
    C) GPS data, detailing exact movement patterns and locations
    D) Both A and B

The correct answer is D:) Both A and B. Although GPS data can be collected, phone records and Internet history are by far the most collected data.

7) What does section 215 of the Foreign Intelligence and Surveillance Act (FISA) require phone carriers and ISPs to do?

    A) Scramble all communications and Internet history records to prevent foreign cybersecurity threats from accessing personal data
    B) Maintain records of all communications and Internet history made with their services
    C) Freely share all information and communications made using their services with governmental agencies
    D) Disclose all instances of specific terminology or phrases being used through their systems to governmental agencies

The correct answer is B:) Maintain records of all communications and Internet history made with their services. FISA requires that all ISPs and phone companies keep records of communications and Internet traffic, but this information can only be utilized under very specific circumstances.

8) When is the NSA lawfully able to access the personal information and communications data that is collected by ISPs and phone companies?

    A) When they are in need of a good laugh by scrolling through silly Google searches
    B) When there is a pressing emergency or threat
    C) When they are granted permission by the FISC based on evidence and probable cause for any major crime
    D) When they are granted permission by the FISC based on evidence and probable cause for national security or suspected terrorism

The correct answer is D:) When they are granted permission by the FISC based on evidence and probable cause for national security or suspected terrorism. One of the major requirements for access to the information collected under FISA is a warrant acquired through the FISC, as well as evidence that the information required is related to a threat to national security or terrorism activities.

9) Which governmental agencies are able to access communications and personal information collected from ISPs and phone providers with the proper warrant?

    A) NSA
    B) CIA
    C) FBI
    D) DEA

The correct answer is A:) NSA. Only the NSA is directly able to access the information collected through FISA, though they have been known to share information with other agencies in some circumstances.

10) True or false: Hacker is a title that refers to criminals who break into computer systems to cause destruction or for personal gain.

    A) True, hackers are all bad
    B) False, not all hackers break the law
    C) Both A and B
    D) None of the above

The correct answer is B:) False, not all hackers break the law. Hacker is simply a term for someone who finds a different way to interact with a technology through the use of specialized knowledge. Hackers can experiment without having to break the law.

11) Which of the following statements is not one of the three principles of hackers as outlined by Herman T. Tavani?

    A) Information should be freely disclosed
    B) Hackers should never disclose security flaws of major systems to the public
    C) Hacking is a useful and important service for society
    D) Activities in cyberspace do not harm real people in the real (physical) world

The correct answer is B:) Hackers should never disclose security flaws of major systems to the public. This option was not among the three principles and is antithetical to the first principle of free information.

12) A hacker going by the name of C00L.D0T performed a cyberattack on a popular video sharing website for the purpose of causing links to child-friendly cartoon videos to instead redirect to scary or disturbing videos. What type of cyberattack would this best be described as?

   A) Access to restricted data
   B) Attack on system resources
   C) Attack on a network
   D) None of the above

The correct answer is C:) Attack on a network. C00L.D0T attacked a system for the purposes of hijacking the entire network to cause widespread chaos.

13) A hacker by the name of dotBOOM! creates a malware program designed to slow infected systems to a crawl by using up the RAM to mine for an online currency and begins spreading it to others through the use of an infected online ad. What type of cyberattack would this best be described as?

   A) Access to restricted data
   B) Attack on system resources
   C) Attack on a network
   D) All of the above

The correct answer is B:) Attack on system resources. The use of a malevolent computer program to utilize a system for a separate task unknown to the user most accurately falls under the definition of an attack on system resources.

14) What is "counter hacking"?

   A) The use of hacking as retribution for a perceived wrong by another
   B) The use of hacking as a form of preventing damage or minimizing damage from another cyberattack
   C) A term used in hacking to describe methods of countering security systems
   D) A term used to describe hackers who work with companies or organizations to improve their online security

The correct answer is B:) The use of hacking as a form of preventing damage or minimizing damage from another cyberattack. Counter hacking is the act of either preventing or minimizing the damage from a malicious hacker, or the retributive act of hacking the hacker back.

15) Is counter hacking an acceptable practice for responding to cyberattacks?

   A) Yes, we have to fight fire with fire
   B) Yes, the UN Charter gives countries the right to respond to attacks, including digital ones
   C) No, the law hasn't found counter hacking to be an acceptable response to cyberattacks because it would mean committing a crime in response to a crime
   D) No, vigilantism is morally reprehensible because it causes more crime

The correct answer is C:) No, the law hasn't found counter hacking to be an acceptable response to cyberattacks because it would mean committing a crime in response to a crime. Digital threats typically need digital responses, but security experts across the board tend to agree that simply responding with a reactionary counter hacking operation could cause more harm than good.

16) What was one of the earliest forms of digital information warfare?

   A) The interception of carrier pigeons in WW1
   B) The use of OCOs in modern conflicts
   C) The information warfare squadrons in the 1980s
   D) The SIGSALY encryption system in WWII

The correct answer is D:) The SIGSALY encryption system in WWII. The SIGSALY computer system allowed for the encryption of wartime information over radio broadcasts, acting as one of the earliest examples of defensive information warfare.

17) During the process of an offensive cyberspace operation (OCO), targeting a military systems computer in a foreign city, the operatives determine that in order to shut down the main systems computer, they would need to overflow the local Internet network and cause it to crash. However, this would also cause several nearby systems to crash as well, including a local hospital. Which of the guiding principles of *jus in bello* could be said to be violated in this operation?

   A) Proportionality
   B) Humanitarianism
   C) Discrimination
   D) Retaliation

The correct answer is C:) Discrimination. Discrimination refers to the belief that warfare should only target systems or locations relevant to military operations, avoiding civilians or necessary infrastructure.

18) Most of the world's leaders agree that cyberwar and cybersecurity should be a priority in discussions of *jus in bello*. What global agreement have they come to?

   A) That UN international law applies to cyberspace
   B) That OCO need to follow the rules outlined in *jus in bello*
   C) Both A and B
   D) None of the above

The correct answer is D:) None of the above. Unfortunately, the world has not yet come to a binding global agreement, though many ideas have been accepted by nations in various combinations.

19) Which is not a reason provided by the opponents of the cyberterrorism label?

   A) Cyberattacks do not currently have the capacity to deal serious real-world damage to inspire terror
   B) There have not yet been enough widescale attacks to warrant its use or to properly define it
   C) The attacks cause panic and can invoke fear and are used to destabilize a society or elements within a society
   D) Both A and B

The correct answer is D:) Both A and B. Although there is a working definition for cyberterrorism, some opponents of the term point to both a lack of effect and a minimal use as a form of attack as being indicators that the term may not be appropriate or needed.

20) Jared was a former IT worker at a large marketing firm. After being laid off for reasons that he believed were not valid, he utilized his (still unchanged) passwords to access and distribute a large amount of personal data that the company had been collecting from customers and caused damage to the internal systems of the company. Based on the provided definition for cyberterrorism, does this example fall under that generally acknowledged definition?

   A) Yes, the attack interfered with the infrastructure of the company
   B) No, the attack was not motivated by a political, religious, or ideological cause
   C) No, the attack was not intended to inspire fear or panic
   D) Yes, the attack utilized cybertechnology

The correct answer is B:) No, the attack was not motivated by a political, religious, or ideological cause. Although the attack may lead to panic from the consumers affected by the breach of information, the driving force of the attack was not ideological in nature, but rather revenge for a perceived personal slight.

21) What is "security theater"?

    A) Actions and measures enforced to provide a feeling of safety that may not actually contribute to better security overall
    B) Effective but public means of enforcing security measures
    C) The use of theater practices to confuse or mislead potential threats to more easily identify and counter them
    D) None of the above

The correct answer is A:) Actions and measures enforced to provide a feeling of safety that may not actually contribute to better security overall. Security theater is a term created to describe the acceptance and enforcement of practices that may not actively improve security but provide an air of safety and perceptions of active action against threats.

CHAPTER III

1) In what instance does "Freedom of Speech" apply?

    A) When the speech is defamatory
    B) When the speech is obscene (by legal standards)
    C) In instances of private action against free speech
    D) In instances of forced or compelled speech

The correct answer is D:) In instances of forced or compelled speech. Under the First Amendment, people are protected from being forced or compelled to speak.

2) Under current legal definition, what is **NOT** used as a measure of obscenity?

    A) Whether the average person with typical standard would consider it indecent
    B) If the material contains sexual conduct displayers in a particularly offensive way
    C) If the material was intended to influence people's minds toward more depraved or corruptive manners
    D) If the material as a whole lacks value, whether artistic, literary, political, or scientific

The correct answer is C:) If the material was intended to influence people's minds toward more depraved or corruptive manners. This measure is based on the Hicklin test, the old measure of obscenity before the introduction of the Roth test.

3) A mayor of a moderately sized city is worried about a political rival in the upcoming election. In an attempt to turn his opponent's support against him, he mischaracterizes a story about his opponent's past and publishes it in a political ad. What could this act be most accurately categorized as?

A) Defamation
B) Slander
C) Libel
D) Both A and B

The correct answer is D:) Both A and B. The published nature of the defamation means that it would specifically be considered libel.

4) Adam Johns is an online celebrity of sorts, known for his show which covers many stories that might typically be considered "conspiracy theories" by most, but are taken very seriously by him and his followers. On his Twitter account, he often makes aggressive and inflammatory posts calling out specific individuals and attacking various groups. One day, Twitter closes his account and informs him that his conduct violated their policies, and that he could no longer use their system. He proclaimed that his "freedom of speech" had been violated. Is Adam correct?

A) Yes, as an American citizen, Adam has a right to express his views
B) No, Twitter is a private company, and has the ability to impose reasonable restrictions on the speech made through their system
C) No, his tweets were obscene and therefore not covered by the First Amendment
D) No, his tweets were defamatory and therefore not covered by the First Amendment

The correct answer is B:) No, Twitter is a private company, and has the ability to impose reasonable restrictions on the speech made through their system. Although often considered a public space, Twitter is a platform owned by a private company, meaning that they are within their rights to restrict an individual's speech if it violated their rules and policies.

5) Which of the following does the U.S. First Amendment **not** have a specific point of non-protection for?

   A) Hate speech
   B) Defamation
   C) Obscenity
   D) Private action against free speech

The correct answer is A:) Hate speech. Unlike many liberal democracies, the U.S. does not have a specific and clear provision against hate speech under its freedom of speech rulings.

6) Although hate speech is technically protected under the First Amendment in the U.S., when does that protection end?

   A) The use of derogatory language against an individual
   B) The use of derogatory language against a group as a whole
   C) The use of speech to incite anger against a specific group
   D) The use of speech to incite unlawful action against a specific group that is likely to be produced

The correct answer is D:) The use of speech to incite unlawful action against a specific group that is likely to be produced. Although there is not a direct provision against hate speech, under certain circumstances, when the speech is attempting to or actively inciting violence, it can be considered criminal.

7) What is privacy legislation?

   A) A set of legal concepts defining who, when, and where people are protected when it comes to privacy
   B) An outline of legal steps required if there was been a violation of privacy
   C) A specified list of what kinds of information can lawfully be collected and shared
   D) All of the above

The correct answer is D:) All of the above. Privacy legislation is an umbrella term covering all of the presented concepts in order to provide a guiding system for dealing with issues of privacy.

8) Holly has two separate email addresses, one for personal use, and one for her job. One day, when logging into her personal email, she notices several emails had been opened, but has no recollection of reading them herself. She checks her account history and sees that there was a login from an unfamiliar IP address and location. The emails that were opened related to her bank account. This is an example of which of the following categories of invasion of privacy?

    A) Intrusion of solitude
    B) Public disclosure of private facts
    C) False light
    D) Appropriation

The correct answer is A:) Intrusion of solitude. For Holly, a digital location was intruded upon without permission with the express purpose of discovering information about her.

9) Timothy is an up-and-coming actor in Hollywood, having appeared in a few moderately successful films. With his success has also come the occasional brush with the paparazzi and the tabloids. One day, he sees his face on the cover image of an online tabloid news list supposing to reveal the strange habits and histories of some of Hollywood's newest stars. Plastered over his image is text reading "Sleeps in an ozone-filled tent at night" and "Caught drunk driving when he was 13," neither of which applied to him, and actually referred to other people on the list. This may be an example of which of the following categories of invasion of privacy?

    A) Intrusion of solitude
    B) Public disclosure of private facts
    C) False light
    D) Appropriation

The correct answer is C:) False light. Timothy has been the subject of malicious misinformation or mischaracterization, though not as directly as, say, a case of defamation.

10) Shanika recently had a video tweet go viral in which she spooks her small pug, causing it to bark loudly. Although most people found the video funny, a small but vocal group responded with anger about her treatment of the dog. One day, she begins receiving multiple aggressive phone calls on her cellphone, and a few days later, notices graffiti on her front door. She soon discovers that some of her personal information had made it online somehow and was being shared around. This is an example of which of the following categories of invasion of privacy?

A) Intrusion of solitude
B) Public disclosure of private facts
C) False light
D) Appropriation

The correct answer is B:) Public disclosure of private facts. For Shanika, information that would generally be considered private has been uncovered trough unlawful means (likely doxing) and exposed to public view.

11) Joseph was a nurse who used to be a competitive weightlifter when he was in college. One day, he notices that his colleagues appear to be giggling as he enters a room. Confused, he asks them what is funny, and they show him an online advertisement for a sports supplement using a photo of him from an old tournament, to which Joseph quickly admits he had no idea about. This is an example of which of the following categories of invasion of privacy?

A) Intrusion of solitude
B) Public disclosure of private facts
C) False light
D) Appropriation

The correct answer is D:) Appropriation. For Joseph, his likeness has been misused without his permission for financial gain (use in an advertisement).

12) Keiko and Keira formed a band when they were in university and have been doing shows for a few years. Recently, they have decided to put out an album online and so decided to file a _____ to protect their ownership of their music. Additionally, they also wanted to get a _____ to protect their band name, "The KK.O.s," as well as the logo that Keira had designed for them from knockoff merchandise should they ever make it big. Which of the below options best completes the above sentences?

   A) Copyright, copyright
   B) Copyright, trademark
   C) Trademark, copyright
   D) Trademark, trademark

The correct answer is B:) Copyright, trademark. A copyright protects a piece of intellectual property, giving ownership to the piece, and providing rights for reproduction and distribution and so would be best used for protecting the individual works of music created by the band. Trademarks protect a branded identity from reproduction or appropriation, so would be best used to protect the name and logo of the band.

13) Under SBCTEA, how many years after the death of an author can something be copyrighted before entering the public domain?

   A) 50 years
   B) 45 years
   C) 60 years
   D) 70 years

The correct answer is D:) 70 years. Although initially only 50 years plus the life of the author, the SBCTEA ruling extended the protection of copyrights to 70 years plus the life of the author.

14) What does it mean if something is in the "public domain"?

   A) The work is widely known among the majority of people
   B) The work is available to the public, but still owned by a copyright holder
   C) The work is publicly available to use, with no copyright restrictions
   D) The work is free from copyright protection but can be repurchased and claimed by another company

The correct answer is C:) The work is publicly available to use, with no copyright restrictions. When a work falls into the public domain, not only does it no longer fall under copyright and can therefore be used freely by the public, but it can also not be re-copyrighted in its original form.

15) Which of the following is not a purpose of the Digital Millennium Copyright Act (DMCA)?

   A) To extend the copyright terms of digital intellectual property
   B) To limit the liability of a company or website for the actions of its users regarding copyright
   C) To allow copyright holders more direct action when it comes to removing unauthorized use of their works
   D) To make P2P file-sharing illegal

The correct answer is D:) To make P2P file-sharing illegal. Although P2P file sharing for the purposes of piracy was sought to be fought against under the DMCA, the act of P2P file-sharing was not banned or made illegal by the bill.

16) Which of the following is not a criterion used by the U.S. Supreme Court when assessing something as being of fair use?

   A) What effect the use would have on the market or value of the copyrighted work
   B) The amount of the copyrighted work that is used
   C) The purpose of the use of the copyrighted work
   D) The medium by which the copyrighted material was utilized

The correct answer is D:) The medium by which the copyrighted material was utilized. The medium through which the copyrighted material is being used is not directly taken into consideration by the Supreme Court when assessing a claim of fair use.

17) Which of the following is not a proposed requirement of the European Union Copyright Directive (EUCD)?

   A) Disallowing links from displaying content without first acquiring a copyright license
   B) Requiring a website to gain permission from a copyright holder before allowing copyrighted works to be uploaded to their platform
   C) Providing the EU with the ability to sue online content distributors and search engines for failing to block copyrighted materials
   D) None of the above

The correct answer is C:) Providing the EU with the ability to sue online content distributors and search engines for failing to block copyrighted materials. This option would have been one of the potential allowances of SOPA and PIPA in the U.S., not the EUCD in the E.U.

18) Which of the following is NOT a form of encryption as discussed in the text?

    A) Asymmetric
    B) End-to-end
    C) Top-to-bottom
    D) Symmetric

The correct answer is C:) Top-to-bottom. Top-to-bottom encryption is not a real form of encryption and was thus not outlined in the text.

19) Roger is doing a master's degree in statistics. One of the most commonly used applications in his program is extremely expensive to buy a license for, and he is unable to acquire one through the school. A friend offers to provide him with a copy of the program, as well as an application that can create a key for it for free. Which cybercrime would be the most applicable in this circumstance?

    A) Phishing
    B) Piracy
    C) Hacking
    D) Cracking

The correct answer is D:) Cracking. Although Roger does technically engage in piracy in acquiring the program, cracking, or the use of a program to circumvent activation code requirements, is the more accurate description of the crime occurring.

20) Tabitha was looking through her emails one day when she noticed an email from PayPal about some unusual activity on her account. Being a small business owner that operated primarily though her online store, Tabitha quickly opened the email and clicked on the link inside, which took her to a login screen. After typing in her account email and password several times, the website still wouldn't accept it. It was then that she noticed the inconsistencies on the page and the website URL, reading paeypal.com. Which cybercrime would be the most applicable in this circumstance?

    A) Malware use
    B) Piracy
    C) Fraud
    D) Phishing

The correct answer is D:) Phishing. Unfortunately for Tabitha, she fell for a phishing scam, having been tricked into providing her information by a duplicitous website.

21) One day, Jeremy sat down at his computer and turned it on, only to find that the computer would not load past the login screen. After several attempts and restarts, it finally got to his desktop, but when it did, a window popped up stating that his computer had been encrypted, and that he would have to send 300 dollars in bitcoin to unlock his computer. Which cybercrime would be the most applicable in this circumstance?

    A) Malware use
    B) Piracy
    C) Hacking
    D) Fraud

The correct answer is A:) Malware use. Jeremy has unfortunately been beset by a piece of malware that has locked his system behind a paywall, meaning that malware use is the most accurate definition for the situation.

CHAPTER IV

1) Fingerprints are an example of what?

    A) Bioinformatics
    B) Genomics
    C) Biometrics
    D) None of the above

The correct answer is C:) Biometrics. More specifically, fingerprints are a kind of physical characteristic that are unique to every individual.

2) Physical characteristic biometrics are unique, so they are a reliable…?

    A) Identifier
    B) Scientific method
    C) Party trick
    D) None of the above

The correct answer is A:) Identifier. Biometrics are often used as authentication methods. For example, using your fingerprint to unlock your phone.

3) Bioinformatics is…?

    A) The mass collection of biometric data
    B) An interdisciplinary field combining computer science, mathematics, and biology
    C) A theoretical model
    D) At-home DNA typing

The correct answer is B:) An interdisciplinary field combining computer science, mathematics, and biology. Bioinformatics has made collecting and analysing different kinds of biological data much easier, resulting in many new breakthroughs.

4) Tony is thinking about trying out a direct-to-consumer genetic testing kit. His friend Charles advises him against it. What is a reason Charles might cite for his position?

    A) Companies sell your data for pharmaceutical tests
    B) DNA data isn't protected under HIPAA
    C) It could drastically change your life to learn about disease risk
    D) All of the above

The correct answer is D:) All of the above. All three statements provide reasonable justification for hesitation to do an at-home DNA test.

5) NFC stands for…?

    A) Non-focused chip
    B) Near-field communication
    C) Not far communication
    D) None of the above

The correct answer is B:) Near-field communication. NFC is the kind of interface used to enable devices to exchange information when they are in close proximity.

6) Muhamad's dog bolted after a squirrel in the park and managed to get lost. Luckily, he has an RFID microchip. How will this help Muhamad recover his dog?

   A) It won't
   B) By enabling Muhamad to track his dog's location
   C) By allowing vets and animal shelters to contact him if they find the dog and scan the RFID chip, which contains Muhamad's name and phone number
   D) None of the above

The correct answer is C:) By allowing vets and animal shelters to contact him if they find the dog and scan the RFID chip, which contains Muhamad's name and phone number. RFID chips can only hold passive data and are activated by the chip reader coming near them.

7) Why is it unreasonable for people to be scared of manipulation and tracking with RFID and NFC microchip implants?

   A) They are just afraid of technological progress in general
   B) Biohackers are really cool people
   C) These kinds of chips contain no internal power source so they can only be activated by the intended mechanism, otherwise they are inert and harmless
   D) None of the above

The correct answer is C:) These kinds of chips contain no internal power source so they can only be activated by the intended mechanism, otherwise they are inert and harmless. GPS trackers need power to be able to communicate with satellites and other related systems.

8) Biohackers believe what?

   A) Direct biological integration with technology is the next stage of human evolution
   B) Everyone should have a microchip
   C) Microchip implants have no place in human biology
   D) None of the above

The correct answer is A:) Direct biological integration with technology is the next stage of human evolution. Biohackers are constantly looking for new ways to safely integrate technology into the human body to explore new kinds of sensations and ideas.

9) What is the Internet of Things (IoT)?

   A) A tech magazine
   B) The concept of Internet addiction
   C) The ability of devices to connect to the Internet and exchange information
   D) None of the above

The correct answer is C:) The ability of devices to connect to the Internet and exchange information. The IoT refers to everything from phones to computers to smart TVs; if it can connect to the Internet, it's in the IoT.

10) Which of the following is a concern over a widespread IoT network?

   A) How to manage informed consent for data collection and sharing
   B) How to prevent bad actors from hacking into major databases filled with so much personal information
   C) How to handle the infrastructure demand of so many devices
   D) All of the above

The correct answer is D:) All of the above. All three statements reflect a reasonable concern to consider for the future of an interconnected IoT network.

11) Which of these is NOT an example of common robotics?

   A) Advanced prosthetic limbs
   B) Automated vacuums
   C) Home security alarm system
   D) Laparoscopic surgery

The correct answer is C:) Home security alarm system. While an alarm system can incorporate some robotic systems, most are just a series of sensors programmed to trigger an alarm if disturbed after activation.

12) Why is it so difficult to program robots and AIs with moral and ethical reasoning?

   A) Programmers can't figure out how
   B) Humans have a wide range of beliefs on ethics and morality that often conflict with each other and finding an acceptable middle ground is difficult
   C) People are worried that robots and AIs will take over the world if they are too advanced
   D) None of the above

The correct answer is B:) Humans have a wide range of beliefs on ethics and morality that often conflict with each other and finding an acceptable middle ground is difficult. To create an acceptable ethical program, people would have to agree on the principles or else the robot would never be allowed to interact outside of a controlled lab.

13) Your smart home device can wish you a good day when you leave for work and can engage in silly banter in response to certain commands. Does this mean your device is sentient?

   A) Yes, it has a personality and can talk to me
   B) Yes, it can take actions and make decisions based on information I give it
   C) No, it is just a machine
   D) No, it doesn't demonstrate self-awareness or independence and can only act based on pre-programmed responses and behaviors

The correct answer is D:) No, it doesn't demonstrate self-awareness or independence and can only act based on pre-programmed responses and behaviors.

14) Which term matches this definition: the entity is self-governing and independent?

   A) Autonomous
   B) Automated
   C) Both A and B
   D) None of the above

The correct answer is A:) Autonomous. Autonomous vehicles, for example, require no direct human input or intervention to function properly once turned on.

15) Which term matches this definition: the entity can perform limited actions independently?

   A) Autonomous
   B) Automated
   C) Both A and B
   D) None of the above

The correct answer is B:) Automated. A device that is automated has limited independent functionality and will typically require some human input to do anything more advanced. Most factory machinery is automated.

16) What is social justice?

   A) A conspiracy to silence free speech
   B) The concept that everyone deserves to be treated fairly and justly
   C) Both A and B
   D) None of the above

The correct answer is B:) The concept that everyone deserves to be treated fairly and justly. Social justice initiatives seek to obtain equality and respect for all.

17) Guy logs into Twitter and sees that a singer he really isn't into has made an inappropriate joke that doesn't upset him, but people are getting angry. Guy decides to join in tweeting angrily at the singer and includes a bunch of nasty hashtags, joining in calls for a boycott of the singer, saying they should just quit social media and apologize for the joke. He logs off feeling vindicated by his actions. What has Guy engaged in?

   A) Outrage culture
   B) Slacktivism
   C) Both A and B
   D) None of the above

The correct answer is C:) Both A and B. Guy has reacted impulsively to a joke that really didn't impact him and felt good about tweeting aggressively at the singer. By engaging in this reactionary and angry behavior, Guy has participated in slacktivism and outrage culture.

CHAPTER V

1) Jeremy was walking home from the grocery store one icy afternoon, and accidentally slipped on a patch of ice on the sidewalk, flinging his bag of groceries at a nearby car on the side of the road. A can of tomatoes dented the door slightly, much to his dismay. He waited for the car's owner to return and offered to pay for part of the repair, blaming the ice for the accident, but still wishing to help. What level of responsibility has Jeremy engaged in with this situation?

    A) Liability
    B) Moral responsibility
    C) Accountability
    D) None of the above

The correct answer is C:) Accountability. Although he has not accepted fault for the accident, nor is he legally being charged for it, he does make steps to assist with the damages that occurred, meaning that he has engaged in accountability.

2) Rick owns a small grocery outlet in a small town. After a particularly rainy few days, a leak begins to appear in the ceiling above one of the aisles, unbeknownst to Rick or his staff. An older customer slips on the forming puddle and injures his hip, requiring him to be rushed to the hospital. A few days later, Rick receives a notice that the man is suing him for damages to cover medical costs. What form of responsibility has occurred in this situation?

    A) Accountability
    B) Moral responsibility
    C) Liability
    D) Both A and B

The correct answer is C:) Liability. Although Rick has not accepted fault for the situation, nor has he indicated accountability, he has been the subject of legal action which, if it goes through, would mean that he is going to be held liable for the incident.

3) Marian is spending time with her good friends Rodger and Michael at their apartment. While there, she accidentally drinks a can of cider, not knowing that Rodger had been saving it for a recipe later that week. She apologises for the mistake and offers to go buy him a new can to replace the one she drank. What form of responsibility has occurred in this situation?

    A) Moral responsibility
    B) Liability
    C) Accountability
    D) Both A and C

The correct answer is D:) Both A and C. Not only did Marian accept personal responsibility for the accident, she also took steps to hold herself accountable by offering to cover the cost of replacing the can.

4) Loo'Roll, a large toilet paper brand, recently released a new toilet paper style which contains a soothing ointment woven into the fibers of the paper. However, in their rush to get the product out to market, they did not properly test the ointment, and have since been inundated with complaints about allergic reactions. The company publicly apologises, pulls the product from the market, and offers to replace all purchased paper with a safer alternative. Additionally, a class action lawsuit has begun building traction, to which the company will likely agree. What form of responsibility has occurred in this situation?

    A) Moral responsibility
    B) Liability
    C) Accountability
    D) All of the above

The correct answer is D:) All of the above. In this circumstance, all three forms of responsibility have been engaged in.

5) Of the three levels of responsibility, which has the credit reporting agency Equifax not yet been full subject to?

    A) Moral Responsibility
    B) Liability
    C) Accountability
    D) All of the above

The correct answer is B:) Liability. Although a class action lawsuit has begun forming, Equifax is actively opposing the action and seeking for the claims to be dismissed. Thus, they have not yet been held liable for the breach.

6) Why is a code of ethical guidelines for IT professionals important?

    A) These individuals have professional knowledge that often cannot be verified by the individuals they are working for/with
    B) These individuals often have access to important systems and personal or private information
    C) Because technology has become increasingly entangled with almost every aspect of our daily lives
    D) All of the above

The correct answer is D:) All of the above. All three presented reasons have been cited as calls for a unified code of ethics among IT professionals.

7) What is a safety-critical system?

    A) A well-made security system
    B) A volatile system
    C) A system that, if tampered with or handled incorrectly, could cause severe damage or harm
    D) None of the above

The correct answer is C:) A system that, if tampered with or handled incorrectly, could cause severe damage or harm. These include air traffic control and mass transit like subway systems.

8) What are the three main purposes of the Gotterbarn Model of IT Ethics?

    A) Ethics, Conduct, and Practice
    B) Accountability, Responsibility, and Action
    C) Excellence, Professionalism, and Quality Service
    D) Improvement, Adaptability, and Perfectionism

The correct answer is A:) Ethics, Conduct, and Practice. According to Gotterbarn, the guideline should support the moral ideals that professionals strive for (ethics), provide codes to guide the behaviour and mental approach to their work (conduct), and direct the work and operations that are unique to the profession and field (practice).

9) Which of the following is not one of the eight key imperatives outlined in the Software Engineering Code of Ethics and Professional Practice (SECEPP)?

   A) Judgment: Software engineers shall maintain integrity and independence in their professional judgment
   B) Self: Software engineers shall participate in lifelong learning regarding the practice of their profession and shall promote an ethical approach to the practice of the profession
   C) Assistance: Software engineers shall, when possible, seek to teach and instruct clients and employers on the most effective uses of their products
   D) Product: Software engineers shall ensure that their products and related modifications meet the highest professional standards possible

The correct answer is C:) Assistance: Software engineers shall, when possible, seek to teach and instruct clients and employers on the most effective uses of their products. According to the SECEPP, IT professionals are not ethically required to teach and instruct their employers or clients.

10) What is a whistle-blower?

   A) Someone who sells sensitive information to news outlets
   B) Someone who likes to complain
   C) Someone who shares sensitive information to bring light to a serious problem
   D) None of the above

The correct answer is C:) Someone who shares sensitive information to bring light to a serious problem. Whistle-blowers break the rules when not doing so would cause serious harm due to the negligence of the higher-ups in their organization.

11) Aliyah is an engineer who works on the automatic subway system in a big city. The software just got an update, but Aliyah is convinced that there is a bug in the new software that could cause two trains to collide at full speed if the right conditions are met. Her supervisors refuse to hear her concerns, claiming that nothing showed up on the simulations. Aliyah smuggles a copy of the software out of the office and gives it to a hacker collective and tells her story to the press. The hackers confirm her suspicions and the problem is fixed, but her employer is trying to fire her. What should she do?

A) Nothing, she should accept the consequences for disobeying her employer
B) Contact OSHA, they can investigate and protect her from wrongful dismissal
C) Sue the employer, if she is going to be fired, she can at least get a better severance package for spotting the problem in the code
D) None of the above

The correct answer is B:) Contact OSHA, they can investigate and protect her from wrongful dismissal. In this case, it is likely that OSHA will find her in the right for her actions and can hold the employer accountable.

12) Tanya covers the local crime beat for an online publication. She submits a story about an 18-year-old man who got kicked out of his home and, after being unable to find a legitimate job, started selling drugs and got caught. She intended for it to be a human-interest piece, but her editor wants her to take a more aggressive angle and really demonize the young man to make the story more enticing. Tanya's gut is telling her that angle would misrepresent the facts of the situation. What journalistic principle is her editor asking Tanya to break?

A) Seek truth and report it
B) Minimize harm
C) Act independently
D) Both A and B

The correct answer is D:) Both A and B. If Tanya rewrites the story, she would no longer be reporting the accurate truth and she could potentially cause this young man some serious harm by ruining his reputation simply to get more clicks.

13) Fredrick is a reporter for a local paper who is writing a story about the potential harms and benefits of a new megastore opening in the town. Word about his involvement in the story has gotten around, as he has received a message from a representative for the megastore not so subtly suggesting that putting more points in the benefits column may come with some benefits for him. If he were to accept the deal, which of the main guiding principles of journalistic ethics would he be violating?

A) Seek truth and report it
B) Minimize harm
C) Act independently
D) Both A and C

The correct answer is D:) Both A and C. In this situation, Fredrick would be failing to seek the truth and report it accurately, and would be influenced by an outside force, so would be failing to act independently, so both A and C are correct.

14) When discussing the ethics of reporting on "fake" or baseless news, which of the four main guiding principles of journalistic ethics would support the decision to report on it?

A) Minimize harm
B) Act independently
C) Seek truth and report it
D) Be accountable

The correct answer is C:) Seek truth and report it. If the goal of an ethical journalist is to seek truth and report it, then they should give time to so-called "fake news" in order to assess its veracity and confirm its falseness for the public.

15) Which journalistic principle could be used to argue against giving too much time to clearly baseless "news"?

A) Minimize harm
B) Seek truth and report it
C) Act independently
D) Be accountable

The correct answer is A:) Minimize harm. Fixation on and repetition of false claims has been shown to actually cause doubt and reduce our ability to accurately judge the credibility of a claim. By moving on quickly, journalists can help minimize harm from their reporting.

16) Jessica firmly believes that the moon landing was a fabrication perpetrated by the U.S. government. While scrolling through her news feed, she ignores a story about the mechanics of the moon landing created by NASA for its anniversary but stops for a video discussing how the zero gravity walk in the video could have been faked in a studio by one of her favorite content creators. What cognitive bias is this an example of?

A) Belief bias
B) Confirmation bias
C) Courtesy bias
D) Distinction bias

The correct answer is B:) Confirmation bias. Confirmation bias is an inherent bias in which humans are more likely to focus on, remember, and agree with material that is consistent with their pre-existing beliefs, which Jessica appears to be doing.

17) Which of these is the correct acronym for the recommended method of seeking out accurate information?

A) CAARP
B) ARCAP
C) CRAAP
D) RAPAC

The correct answer is C:) CRAAP. It stands for currency, relevance, authority, accuracy, and purpose. Keeping these in mind will help you be more aware of bias in claims and reports.

18) Who bears the responsibility for preventing the spread of misinformation online?

A) Journalists
B) Website hosts and providers
C) The users
D) All of the above

The correct answer is D:) All of the above. Everyone on the Internet shares responsibility for doing their part to encourage education and critical thinking to help stop the spread of misinformation and falsehoods.

19) Which of the following is one of the reasons some people oppose net neutrality laws?

    A) ISPs want to charge more to impress investors
    B) They don't believe the Internet is important enough to be considered a utility
    C) ISPs want to impose their own ethics and morals on consumers
    D) ISPs are forced to charge companies who use a significant amount of bandwidth an amount reasonably compared to regular users, which results in disproportionate pricing

The correct answer is D:) ISPs are forced to charge companies who use a significant amount of bandwidth an amount reasonably compared to regular users, which results in disproportionate pricing. While some people believe the other options are also reasons for opposing net neutrality, it is unlikely any ISP would openly admit it. Disproportionate prices, however, is a valid concern.

20) Which of the following is not a statute of the recently repealed net neutrality laws in the U.S.?

    A) ISPs were blocked from introducing additional paywalls into the use of their networks
    B) Payment for use of the network based on levels of bandwidth use, with larger use companies paying significantly more
    C) Classifying the Internet as a utility, akin to water or power
    D) Maintaining a level playing field for both large companies and small business and individuals online

The correct answer is B:) Payment for use of the network based on levels of bandwidth use, with larger use companies paying significantly more. Under the former net neutrality laws, large bandwidth users like large companies were not charged on a different pay-scale compared to the average consumer.

🎓 *Test-Taking Strategies*

Here are some test-taking strategies that are specific to this test and to other DSST tests in general:

- Keep your eyes on the time. Pay attention to how much time you have left.

- Read the entire question and read all the answers. Many questions are not as hard to answer as they may seem. Sometimes, a difficult sounding question really only is asking you how to read an accompanying chart. Chart and graph questions are on most DANTES/DSST tests and should be an easy free point.

- If you don't know the answer immediately, the new computer-based testing lets you mark questions and come back to them later if you have time.

- Read the wording carefully. Some words can give you hints to the right answer. There are no exceptions to an answer when there are words in the question such as always, all or none. If one of the answer choices includes most or some of the right answers, but not all, then that is not the answer. Here is an example:

  The primary colors include all of the following:
     A) Red, Yellow, Blue, Green
     B) Red, Green, Yellow
     C) Red, Orange, Yellow
     D) Red, Yellow, Blue

  Although item A includes all the right answers, it also includes an incorrect answer, making it incorrect. If you didn't read it carefully, was in a hurry, or didn't know the material well, you might fall for this.

- Make a guess on a question that you do not know the answer to. There is no penalty for an incorrect answer. Eliminate the answer choices that you know are incorrect. For example, this will let your guess be a 1 in 3 chance instead.

🎓 *Test Preparation*

How much you need to study depends on your knowledge of a subject area. If you are interested in literature, took it in school, or enjoy reading then your study and preparation for the literature or humanities test will not need to be as intensive as that of someone who is new to literature.

This book is much different than the regular DANTES study guides. This book actually teaches you the information that you need to know to pass the test. If you are particularly interested in an area, or feel that you want more information, do a quick search online. We've tried not to include too much depth in areas that are not as essential on the test. Everything in this book will be on the test. It is important to understand all major theories and concepts listed in the table of contents. It is also important to know any bolded words.

Don't worry if you do not understand or know a lot about the area. With minimal study, you can complete and pass the test.

Legal Note

FLASHCARDS

This section contains flashcards for you to use to further your understanding of the material and test yourself on important concepts, names or dates. Read the term or question then flip the page over to check the answer on the back. Keep in mind that this information may not be covered in the text of the study guide. Take your time to study the flashcards, you will need to know and understand these concepts to pass the test.

Password	**Captcha code**
Bots	**Encryption**
Plaintext	**Cipher**
Firewall	**Malware**

A program or system intended to distinguish human from machine input, typically as a way of thwarting spam and automated extraction of data from websites

A string of characters that allows access to a computer system or service

The process of converting information or data into a code, especially to prevent unauthorized access

Digital programs designed to act as real individuals online

A secret or disguised way of writing; a code

Text that is not computationally tagged, specially formatted, or written in code

Harmful software

A system that acts as a checkpoint between trusted and untrusted sources and your device

Trojan virus

Authentication

VPN

Norms of appropriateness

Norms of distribution

Contextual integrity

Privacy policy

Netiquette

The process or action of verifying the identity of a user or process

A program designed to breach the security of a computer system while ostensibly performing some innocuous function

Determines what types of information are or are not appropriate for a given context

A method employing encryption to provide secure access to a remote computer over the Internet

A theory of privacy developed by professor Helen Nissenbaum

Restricts or limits the flow of information within and across contexts

Proper online behavior

A document that explains how an organization handles any customer, client or employee information gathered in its operations

Online code of conduct

Ad blocker

Meme

Influencer

Native advertising

Psychological ownership theory

Outrage culture

Data mining

A piece of software designed to prevent advertisements from appearing on a web page

A collection of rules and regulations that include what is and is not acceptable or expected behavior

A person with the ability to influence potential buyers of a product or service by promoting or recommending the items on social media

A humorous image, video, piece of text, etc., that is copied (often with slight variations) and spread rapidly by Internet users

Claims that humans have a natural urge to collect and accumulate things

Any instance in which an advertisement takes the form of the typically expected content on an online platform, potentially disguising its true nature as an advertisement

The practice of examining large databases in order to generate new information

The social phenomenon of publicly denouncing perceived racism, sexism, homophobia, transphobia, classism, national interest, and other forms of bigotry

Communications Assistance for Law Enforcement Act (CALEA)

PRISM

Data-driven marketing

Explicit data

Implicit data

Internet cookies

Hacker

Counter hacking

Requires U.S. Internet providers to hand over data pertaining to specified searches to the NSA

Requires all U.S. telecommunications providers to make their system easy to tap if law enforcement deem it necessary to gather intel on suspected criminals and typically requires that they obtain a warrant to set up the wiretap

Information that is clear and stated directly

The practice of collecting and analyzing consumer data to gather insights to guide marketing and brand decisions

Track your activity on the website (what pages you visit, how long you spend on them, the links you click, and files you download) and store this information in a file on your computer

Conclusions suggested by patterns in the rest of the information

The act of engaging in hacker activities to either prevent an attack or to attack back

A person who uses computers to gain unauthorized access to data

IP spoofing

Offensive cyberspace operation (OCO)

SIGSALY

jus bellum justum

jus in bello

Cyberterrorism

Security theater

Slander

A mission that takes the form of gathering tactical information (often via interception and decryption of confidential foreign communications), the dissemination of propaganda, or disinformation for the purposes of demoralization or manipulation

The act of hijacking another person's device IP address and using it as a cloak over your own

Just war theory; refers to the set of general understandings and criteria that humans have explicitly or implicitly agreed are the "ethical standards" for wars

A speech encipherment system used in WW2 that was enormous (spanning 2,000 square feet) and had to be operated in a certain temperature range because there was so much sensitive equipment involved

An act committed via the Internet with the intention of achieving some political or ideological goal

The law in waging war; discrimination and proportionality

A spoken action of defamation

The practice of investing in countermeasures intended to provide the feeling of improved security while doing little or nothing to achieve it

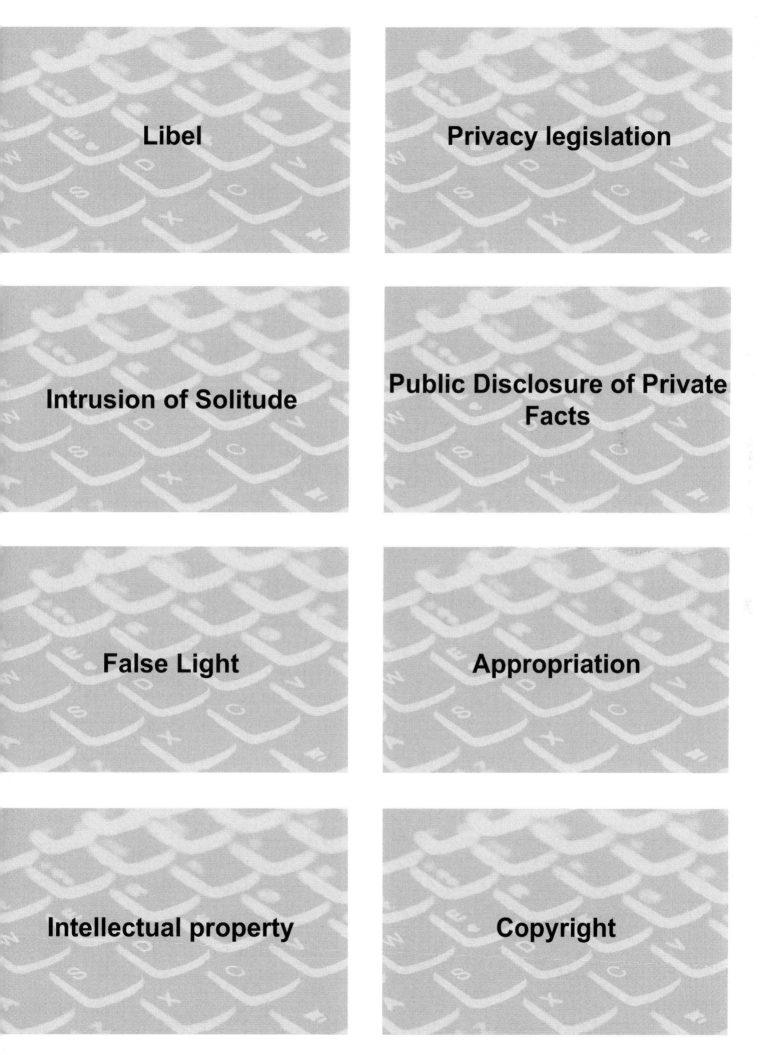

Libel

Privacy legislation

Intrusion of Solitude

Public Disclosure of Private Facts

False Light

Appropriation

Intellectual property

Copyright

A series of interconnected legal concepts that are applied in a variety of contexts

The publication of the slanderous material

The sharing of personal information that is truthful which most reasonable people would consider to be an objectionable action

An intentional intrusion into one's private quarters, physical or electronic

Using a person's name or likeness without permission to acquire some sort of benefit

The sharing of false (though not necessarily defamatory) facts which cause others to view a person in a false light

Automatically given to the author or creator of any fixed piece of work and can be legally ratified by applying to the United States Copyright Office. When you have copyright over a piece of work, you have the power to republish the work in part or in whole, sell or give licenses to others to do the same (and revoke them), and you can pursue legal action against someone if they recreate your work without your permission

Any intangible object created by an individual or group that belongs to them according to generally accepted copyright laws and norms

Made in the
USA
Columbia, SC